⊄⫴B The Practitioner's Bookshelf

Hands-On Language and Literacy Books for
Classroom Teachers and Administrators

Dorothy S. Strickland
FOUNDING EDITOR, LANGUAGE AND LITERACY SERIES

Celia Genishi and Donna E. Alvermann
LANGUAGE AND LITERACY SERIES EDITORS*

Literacy Instruction in Multilingual Classrooms:
Engaging English Language Learners in Elementary School
Lori Helman

RTI and the Adolescent Reader:
Responsive Literacy Instruction in Secondary Schools
William G. Brozo

Let's Poem:
The Essential Guide to Teaching Poetry in a High-Stakes, Multimodal World
Mark Dressman

Literacy in the Welcoming Classroom:
Creating Family–School Partnerships That Support Student Learning
JoBeth Allen

DIY Media in the Classroom: New Literacies Across Content Areas
Barbara Guzzetti, Kate Elliott, and Diana Welsch

Bring It to Class: Unpacking Pop Culture in Literacy Learning
Margaret C. Hagood, Donna E. Alvermann, and Alison Heron-Hruby

The Reading Turn-Around: A Five-Part Framework for Differentiated Instruction
Stephanie Jones, Lane W. Clarke, and Grace Enriquez

Academic Literacy for English Learners:
High-Quality Instruction Across Content Areas
Cynthia Brock, Diane Lapp, Rachel Salas, and Dianna Townsend

Literacy for Real: Reading, Thinking, and Learning in the Content Areas
ReLeah Cossett Lent

Teaching Individual Words: One Size Does Not Fit All
Michael F. Graves

Literacy Essentials for English Language Learners: Successful Transitions
Maria Uribe and Sally Nathenson-Mejía

Literacy Leadership in Early Childhood: The Essential Guide
Dorothy S. Strickland and Shannon Riley-Ayers

* For a list of current titles in the Language and Literacy Series, see *www.tcpress.com*

Literacy Instruction in Multilingual Classrooms

ENGAGING ENGLISH LANGUAGE LEARNERS
IN ELEMENTARY SCHOOL

LORI HELMAN

Foreword by Alison L. Bailey

Teachers College, Columbia University
New York and London

Published by Teachers College Press, 1234 Amsterdam Avenue, New York, NY 10027

Library of Congress Cataloging-in-Publication Data

Helman, Lori.
    Literacy instruction in multilingual classrooms : engaging English language learners in
        elementary school / Lori Helman ; foreword by Alison Bailey.
            p. cm. — (The practitioners' bookshelf)
    Includes bibliographical references and index.
    ISBN 978-0-8077-5336-1 (pbk.)
        1. English language—Study and teaching (Elementary)—Foreign speakers.
    I. Title.
    PE1128.A2H3954   2012
    372.652'1—dc23   2011049957

ISBN 978-0-8077-5336-1 (paper)

Printed on acid-free paper
Manufactured in the United States of America

19 18 17 16 15 14 13 12   8 7 6 5 4 3 2 1

Contents

Foreword

It was a delight to see the word *multilingual* in the title of Lori Helman's new book on literacy instruction. In an era when bilingual education has been used as a political tool, educators can move beyond the frustrations of opposing sides and empty rhetoric to focus on new realities, including the fact that many children throughout the United States come to school already speaking two or more languages. Frequently classrooms comprise not just two languages in contact but, as the voices of the teachers in this book will attest, any given classroom today can be home to a large variety of different languages.

School districts in the United States can encounter up to 90 different languages spoken by enrolled students. At the state level, there may be well over 200 different languages represented in the K–12 population. Here are the top ten languages spoken at home by U.S. residents after English, in descending order of frequency: Spanish, a specific Chinese dialect, Vietnamese, Korean, Tagalog, Russian, French Creole, Arabic, Portuguese or Portuguese Creole, and one of several African languages (Pandya, McHugh, & Batalova, 2011). According to the U.S. Census Bureau (April, 2010), over 55 million U.S. residents over the age of 5 years speak a language other than English at home. This number does not take into consideration the 30 million U.S. children under age 5 who are currently growing up in households where languages other than or in addition to English are being spoken.

These children have the potential to speak more than one language, and, importantly, if their schools and classroom teachers can support them appropriately, they also have a valuable opportunity to learn to read and write in more than one language. However, as Lori Helman reports, a shocking 91% of elementary schools offer their English language learners English-speaking only environments for content instruction.

What can teachers in these environments do? Certainly, it is time for those who educate teachers and those who employ teachers to acknowledge this reality and provide teachers with the wherewithal to engage their multilingual students in effective literacy instruction. Lori Helman is well positioned to help in this crucial enterprise. She has been an elementary bilingual teacher as well as a teacher educator. As a university researcher, she has traced the development of literacy in young English language learners by looking at the influence of several factors, including a child's first language. Moreover, Helman has collaborated with various colleagues to develop materials for literacy instruction based on research findings with English language learners.

The value of the book is how it can enable teachers to learn about their multilingual students in ways that effectively help students learn. The chapters systematically take the reader on a tour of the terrain to establish important relationships among literacy, community, and engagement. A succession of topics provide the underlying principles and strategies for forging connections with families, building on first language literacy, adopting informal assessment approaches, and making explicit the linguistic, cognitive, and sociocultural demands inherent in reading and writing activities. The end result provides a thorough treatment of how to create a multilingual and multifaceted classroom community, how to support literacy development and its assessment, and how to accomplish all this while engaging students, families, and colleagues in robust literacy instruction.

This new book can serve as the core text of a teacher preparation course, but I believe it will be most welcomed and most effectively used again and again as a reference by current classroom teachers. This is an important distinction to draw, because it is frequently the case that not until teachers acquire their own classrooms do they recognize the necessity for a deep understanding of the language-based experiences and development of students. This book is Lori Helman's gift to those teachers. She speaks directly to the reader, making the book particularly accessible to educators looking to independently increase their knowledge base and expand their reach with all students.

Alison L. Bailey
Professor of Education
University of California, Los Angeles

REFERENCE

Pandya, C., McHugh, M., & Batalova, J. (2011). *Limited English proficient individuals in the United States: Number, share, growth, and linguistic diversity.* Washington, DC: Migration Policy Institute.

Acknowledgments

This book is a reflection of years of teaching, mentoring, and researching experiences in multilingual classrooms. I am grateful to all of the students, families, and colleagues who have guided my way through these more than 30 years in education. Each idea, story, or vignette is based on students, teachers, and other school leaders who have been a part of my journey in elementary school teaching. First, I'd like to thank the young students who, throughout my career and to this day, continue to make teaching the most amazing and touching profession I could hope to be a part of. I especially thank the students and families who have allowed me to study and document their literacy-learning journey from first through sixth grade over the past 6 years. I have learned so much from you. I also want to thank the teachers who fit me into their high-speed schedules to think together, observe students, and plan for how classroom teaching will evolve in changing times. I know you are busy and overloaded, and I very much appreciate your willingness to share your classrooms and ideas with me.

As I wrote this book I had a chance to reflect on the excellent mentors with whom I have worked in my career—the "just in time" coaches who helped me learn to set up positive classroom guidelines or understand the heart of students' literacy development. I thank you all for the gifts you give to teachers every day, and I hope that in a similar way this book serves to mentor teachers in their journey of continuous learning.

I'd like to thank the university research assistants who have supported my work with students and families over the past 7 years in higher education. In particular, thanks go to Carrie Rogers and Maggie Struck for their enthusiasm, detailed data collection, and positive attitude with students, families, and educators. Finally, I wish to thank Amy Frederick, research fellow and doctoral candidate, for the incredible support I received from her. When I came to the Midwest, Amy introduced me to many teachers and schools in my new home. She worked with me on research studies in schools, co-authored a number of papers and presentations, and shared her ideas and background experiences as an ELL teacher. Amy helped on the book in several ways, including reading first drafts of manuscripts and contributing classroom photos.

I send this text out into the world with much appreciation for the efforts of educators and families who stay focused on creating supportive and engaging communities for children.

Literacy Instruction in Multilingual Classrooms

ENGAGING ENGLISH LANGUAGE LEARNERS
IN ELEMENTARY SCHOOL

Introduction

> "I have 15 different languages represented by the students in my classroom.
> I can't possibly differentiate instruction based on students' language backgrounds."

WELCOME TO *Literacy Instruction in Multilingual Classrooms: Engaging English Language Learners in Elementary School*. Maybe you have picked this book up because you are an elementary teacher whose classroom community is rich with cultural and linguistic diversity. Or possibly you have students in your classroom who are developing oral proficiency in English and you are searching for tools to help them flourish. In either case, you have come to the right place. This book is designed to be a hands-on resource that elementary teachers can pull off the shelf to get quick access to important ideas in a brief format. Each chapter contains important information in a stand-alone format, and throughout the book there are lots of charts, figures, and photographs to make the content easy to access and understand.

In this book you will find key ideas about community building, language development, and literacy learning and teaching with multilingual students. In the chapters that follow, I will discuss how to learn and build on the diverse linguistic resources that students bring to school, the connection between oral language and literacy development, how reading and writing skills develop for second language learners, assessing language and literacy learning, planning literacy curriculum for classrooms with students from many language backgrounds, and how to collaborate with other professionals to coordinate effective instruction for students.

My goal is for you to use the book as a reference for the specific questions you have about organizing language-enriched literacy instruction in a multilingual community. Chapter 1 is an introduction to the key ideas addressed in the book and will serve as your roadmap for navigating the chapters that follow. Chapter 2 shares ideas for organizing the physical environment of your classroom, setting up routines and procedures, and involving family members. Chapter 3 addresses the important challenge of providing oral language development, including academic English. Chapter 4 outlines how readers progress through the developmental levels, illustrated by one student's journey over his elementary career. Chapter 5 explains how reading and writing work together, and I share one immigrant student's progress from emergent to intermediate development.

Chapter 6 provides examples of tools teachers can use to informally assess the language abilities of their students, an important aspect of developing a language-rich classroom. The chapter also provides an overview of the different purposes of various kinds of assessment. In Chapter 7 I focus on vocabulary and academic language development. I share examples of lessons from three elementary teachers who explicitly teach academic language as part of their reading and writing lessons. Chapter 8 reviews what effective instruction for students learning English looks like. I compile examples from activities in other chapters in the book to highlight effective instructional practices. At the end of the book, a brief resource section points you to some useful websites for further exploration. Many examples from real classrooms and students are shared throughout the book. Students are given pseudonyms to maintain their anonymity.

As you can see, this book covers a lot of ground and is packed with practical information in an easy-to-access format. I hope this book will be a useful gateway to your next steps in building an engaging multilingual community for literacy learning.

CHAPTER I

Knowledge for Teaching ALL Students to Read and Write

THE STUDENTS in Carrie's third-grade classroom come from a number of language backgrounds, ethnic groups, and homelands. Some of the students were born in the United States to immigrant parents, while others are more recent arrivals to the country, including some who are refugees from war and famine. Carrie has a number of bilingual students whose families have lived for several generations in the United

> In 2007–08, 71.7% of all elementary schools had at least one student classified as *limited English proficient*, a term used by the U.S. Department of Education to describe students still learning English (Aud et al., 2010).
>
> Of the total elementary school population, 14.1% were classified as limited English proficient (Aud et al., 2010).
>
> One in five students in prekindergarten to 12th grade in the year 2000 was the child of an immigrant, and the number has continued to grow (Capps, Fix, Murray, Ost, Passel, & Herwantoro, 2005).

States. Some of Carrie's students come from homes where English is the only spoken language, and they have varying levels of vocabulary skills and diverse social, educational, and cultural backgrounds. This year, Carrie has six different language groups represented in her class. Although she speaks only English, Carrie feels that each new student who enrolls in her class teaches her more and more about world languages and their distribution across the globe!

Carrie wonders, "How can I possibly differentiate my instruction to address the variety of languages and backgrounds among the students in my class?" Also, "Do my students' language backgrounds influence what I will need to teach them so they can become capable readers and writers?" Despite the great variation of language and literacy skills that her students bring to third grade, Carrie is committed to—and held responsible for—making sure that every student achieves the district standards. Often this goal energizes her; on other days, however, the task feels overwhelming.

Carrie's third-grade classroom is representative of a growing number of teaching contexts across the country. In big cities, small cities, suburbs, and rural environments alike, classrooms are becoming increasingly diverse in many ways, including, for example, students' home languages and ethnicities, cultural backgrounds, and academic skills.

Data for pre-K through fifth-grade classrooms show that the vast majority (76.1%) of limited-English-proficient children speak Spanish as a first language (Capps et al., 2005). The top 10 languages spoken by limited-English-proficient students in these grade levels are Spanish, Chinese,

Top 10 Languages

Spanish
Chinese
Vietnamese
Korean
Hmong/Miao
French
German
Russian
French/Haitian Creole
Arabic (Capps et al., 2005)

> Data from the 2009 National Assessment of Educational Progress show that:
>
> 1. Seventy-one percent of fourth-grade students classified as English language learners (ELL) fell below the basic level in reading (as compared with 30% of students who are not ELL).
> 2. The average reading score of an ELL student in fourth grade was 188, 36 points lower than the 224 average score of a student who was not ELL. (U.S. Department of Education, 2010)

Vietnamese, Korean, Hmong/Miao, French, German, Russian, French/Haitian Creole, and Arabic.

In districts like Carrie's, there are sometimes 60 languages or more spoken in the students' homes and communities. In addition to students who speak Spanish, Hmong, and Vietnamese, Carrie's district has many students who speak Somali, Oromo, and Laotian. In this multilingual setting, it is Carrie's goal to create a collaborative learning community that engages in language-rich literacy experiences and makes accelerated progress in mastering the challenging grade-level expectations.

SETTINGS AND PROGRAMS FOR ENGLISH LEARNERS

A variety of structures exist in elementary schools for English learners. Some schools work to find bilingual teachers and language resources in students' home languages and strive to offer the sort of bilingual programs that have been found to be highly effective in helping students become literate both in English and in their primary languages (Genesee, Lindholm-Leary, Saunders, & Christian, 2005; Thomas & Collier, 2002). Other programs include transitional bilingual programs that teach students to read and write in a home language first, and then help them transfer those skills into English literacy learning over a period of several years. In some schools English learners are assessed on their English-speaking abilities and then given support services from an English language development teacher either by being pulled out of their classroom (pull-out instruction) or by having services delivered within the classroom (push-in instruction).

There is great variation across communities, both in the methods used to identify students as limited English proficient (LEP) and in determining which students receive services and what those services consist of. Depending on the total number of English learners in a given school or district, often only the students with the most limited spoken English skills are given special services. Schools that have LEP students are asked to describe the characteristics of their programs by the Department of Education; data from the 2003–04 school year for elementary schools show that:

- 85.7% use regular English-speaking classrooms to teach English
- 90.8% use regular English-speaking classrooms to teach other subjects
- Only 15.8% of elementary school programs use the students' home languages to teach other subjects (U.S. Department of Education, 2004).

So, for the large majority of students who are learning English, the primary mode of delivery is in the regular, English-speaking classroom. It is easy to see how English learners may get "lost in the crowd" in the hectic world of an all-English classroom, and how they could come to feel like they are "drowning" in a sea of English.

LEARNING NEW NAMES AND NEW WAYS TO TEACH

Over her 9 years of teaching, Carrie has been introduced to students, families, and communities that were previously unfamiliar to her. Her students' names now include Yuli, Pao, Mohamed, and Tuan, and each name and child springs from the diverse cultural group to which he or she belongs. Names are only a small part of a cultural identity, but they are symbolic of the changes occurring in the demographics of elementary schools across the United States and in numerous other countries. What adaptations to teaching practice will be needed to best serve all students in the increasingly diverse elementary classroom? How will students' language background skills and proficiency in English be taken into account when constructing lessons and choosing content? What new ways of teaching will Carrie and other educators need in order to teach all students to become literate in English? The following key ideas introduce important teacher knowledge for creating effective literacy instruction with English learners. These topics are highlighted and revisited throughout the book in individual chapters.

CREATING A MULTILINGUAL CLASSROOM COMMUNITY

Community gives people a sense of belonging and power, and it provides them with a means to meet their needs and form an emotional connection to a group (Chavis, Hogge, McMillan, & Wandersman, 1986). Ideally, we all are more motivated and feel safer, more competent, and more connected when we work within a community.

What happens if teachers do not structure a classroom community where all students, including those who speak languages other than English, feel valued and included? English learners may begin to feel that they do not belong. They may wonder whether they are expected to participate or master the curriculum (Au, 2009). Students may come to feel that the school community does not understand them, and that they cannot truly be themselves in the classroom. Students may become embarrassed about their home language and culture if the school is not welcoming or under-

LINKS TO OTHER CHAPTERS IN THIS BOOK

Chapter 2 describes effective practices in creating a multilingual classroom community such as:

- Accepting students' attempts to communicate in their home language
- Explicitly celebrating the diversity of languages present in the classroom
- Using collaborative learning structures
- Conducting teacher-led, small-group instruction
- Matching activities to students' cultural backgrounds
- Holding high expectations for student learning
- Finding out what students know in a home language so that connections can be made to literacy learning in English (Au, 2009)

standing of its features. In the end, students may believe that they need to choose between who they are in their home environment, and the kind of person who is accepted at school.

Teachers may assume that the learning environment they have created at school is equally welcoming for all students, regardless of their cultural or linguistic background. Teachers may miss the differences among their students' various cultures, including differences in styles of social interaction, the acceptable roles of adults and children at home, collaborative versus competitive outlooks on achievement, or approved motivations and goals for individuals. To ensure that all students feel emotionally connected and are held to the same high expectations, teachers will need to become more conscious of the ways they develop a community that is inclusive of all students in the class.

BUILDING ON THE LANGUAGES OF FAMILIES AND COMMUNITIES

Families are an essential resource for developing literacy with English learners. Not only are families most children's first teachers, but they also can motivate children to read and write, provide opportunities for children to practice and apply what they learn in school, give children an audience for their writing and literacy explorations, and provide information about children's literacy in their home languages. Families and community members serve as a window into how literacy is used in meaningful ways in students' neighborhoods and cultural communities.

If an effort is not made by the teacher and school to connect with students' families, students may come to see literacy at school as separate from their real-world lives outside of school. Also, families who otherwise might be interested in supporting their children's success in school may feel unimportant or not included if the school does not reach out to them. This takes away an important source of support for the academic program and students' evolution into lifelong readers and writers.

Teachers may not understand the powerful relationship between students' success at school and the involvement of their families. They may feel too busy to make connections to their students' families and com-

---

LINKS TO OTHER CHAPTERS IN THIS BOOK

Chapter 2 describes effective practices in building on the languages of families and communities such as:

- Developing partnerships with families to provide information about out-of-school literacy practices
- Connecting those practices to literacy inside the classroom
- Communicating school information to families in creative, accessible ways
- Visiting the homes and community events of students to learn about the diverse cultural values and experiences of students
- Recruiting the help of a community liaison to translate parents' ideas about schooling
- Researching students' languages and literacy practices to better understand their specific reading and writing behaviors (Allen, 2010)

---

munities, or they may be worried about the responses they may get if they reach out from the classroom. To ensure that students are making the most of literacy instruction at school, it is critical for teachers to be inclusive of the families, communities, and literacy practices of their students (Gonzáles, Moll, & Amanti, 2005).

PLANNING FOR AND IMPLEMENTING LANGUAGE-ENRICHED INSTRUCTION

Language is how we as people communicate and share our ideas. It is how we give meaning to what we think about. Language is core to everything that school attempts to accomplish, from learning a new skill to understanding a complex theory. Whether the task is as simple as learning a new sight word or as thoughtful as tracking a character's development in a piece of literature, students call upon their language competencies.

If teachers ignore the language demands of literacy tasks in school, English learners may struggle to keep up with what is going on in class. Even if students are able to understand some of the content, they may

---

LINKS TO OTHER CHAPTERS IN THIS BOOK

Chapters 3 and 7 describe the importance of oral language development and embedding language into literacy instruction such as:

- Examining the language requirements of the reading, writing, listening, and speaking tasks in which students engage
- Identifying how the language demands build on or challenge students' current levels of English proficiency
- Connecting the new language to what students are already able to do
- Explicitly sharing the vocabulary and language features that students will need to know to make sense of the academic task at hand (Dutro & Helman, 2009)

LINKS TO OTHER CHAPTERS IN THIS BOOK

Chapter 4 outlines reading development and how teachers can support its progress in a multilingual learning community by:

- Finding out about students' home languages and how they are similar to or different from the academic English used in class
- Informally assessing students' reading skills in the home language and building on that knowledge in English-reading instruction
- Explicitly clarifying confusions that exist between the sound systems of a student's home language and the English used in class
- Focusing on key vocabulary and language structures that will help students to access the text
- Keeping meaning paramount so that students do not come to see reading as a rote process that does not involve making mindful connections

not be aware of important key concepts. Students may feel that school is not making sense, or they may try to "get by" through mimicking what others do without really understanding why they're doing it. They may learn to decode individual words, but they may not comprehend them or be able to use them in speech or writing. They may struggle at the word, sentence, or text level as they engage with the school curriculum (Bailey & Heritage, 2008).

Teachers may perceive their English-learning students as being more proficient than they actually are. Many students have a conversational competence in English but lack the academic language necessary to understand the more formal vocabulary and syntactic structures that they encounter in their texts or in classroom lectures (Cummins, 1981; Schleppegrell, 2004). To ensure that all students are able to profit from instruction, teachers can learn to take into account the language demands of classroom tasks, including unfamiliar vocabulary, text style, language function, complex sentence structures, idiomatic expressions (e.g., *in the same boat*), and the role of transitional phrases (e.g., *nevertheless, on the other hand, in contrast*).

UNDERSTANDING ENGLISH LEARNERS' READING DEVELOPMENT

Reading development is a complex process that builds on language development, concepts of print, phonemic awareness, effortless decoding, and extracting meaning from text (Pressley, 2006). While students generally progress in their reading development in fairly predictable ways, it is important to understand the differences for students who are learning to read an unfamiliar language at the same time they are learning to speak and understand it. When students know a large body of words in English, it facilitates their ability to hear similar sounds across those words and helps them to comprehend those words as they are encountered in text.

LINKS TO OTHER CHAPTERS IN THIS BOOK

Chapter 5 outlines writing development and how teachers can support its progress in a multilingual learning community by:

- Learning more about students' home languages
- Finding out about the writing and storytelling practices used in students' homes
- Incorporating these practices into the classroom curriculum
- Reading students' writing samples to informally assess confusions in phonology, syntax, and vocabulary
- Building on home language literacy skills
- Providing models in English
- Guiding the writing process
- Using writing to communicate with others in meaningful ways

---

When students are comfortable differentiating the specific sounds in English, this supports their development of letter–sound relationships. For English learners who are still developing this linguistic knowledge, the path to proficient reading development is more complex than for native speakers.

What happens if teachers do not understand the differences in reading development for students learning English? In class, students learning the academic English of the classroom may be able to decode words, but they might not comprehend what they are reading. They may struggle with phonics because of the subtle differences in sounds across vowels and consonants that do not exist in their home languages. Students may not be able to bring foundational preliteracy skills from their home languages to buoy them in learning to read in English.

Teachers may assume that reading development is the same for all students, whether or not they are native speakers of a language. They may not understand the vocabulary, phonological, syntactic, and pragmatic confusions that could stymie students' progress in reading. To ensure that all students make progress toward becoming accomplished readers, teachers can learn about reading development for native speakers of a language and then investigate the complexities of this process for students who are learning the academic English of the classroom.

UNDERSTANDING ENGLISH LEARNERS' WRITING DEVELOPMENT

Writing and spelling development go hand-in-hand with reading development. As they write individual words and encode their complete thoughts into text, students pull from the same pool of knowledge they use while reading. Just as reading development is more complex for English learners, so is writing development. Students may confuse letter–sound repre-

> **LINKS TO OTHER CHAPTERS IN THIS BOOK**
>
> Chapter 6 describes key informal assessment practices to help teachers better understand students' language and literacy development such as:
> - Making ongoing assessment an integral part of the instructional process (Lipson & Wixson, 2009)
> - Providing students with frequent opportunities to show what they are learning
> - Discussing students' (mis)conceptions
> - Receiving adapted instruction as necessary
> - Using a menu of informal, classroom-based activities that are most critical for assessing students' reading and writing skills at each of the developmental reading levels

sentations if there are discrepancies between the sound systems of English and their home languages, regardless of whether they have had formal literacy instruction in a first language. Students may need support to express their ideas in English if their language skills are limited.

What happens if teachers do not understand the differences in writing development for students learning English? Students may use sound–symbol representations that reflect phonetic understandings from their home languages. Students may feel overwhelmed by the attempt to put together the planning tasks, encoding skills needed, vocabulary resources, and language structures that work together to write connected text.

Teachers may assume that writing development is the same for all students, whether or not they are native speakers of a language, or that the process is the same for all English learners. They may not understand the vocabulary, phonological, syntactic, and pragmatic confusions that may complicate students' progress in writing. Teachers may undervalue students' narrative constructions that are related to cultural sharing styles (McCabe, 1997). To ensure that all students make progress toward becoming accomplished writers, teachers can learn about writing development for native speakers of a language and then investigate the complexities of this process for English learners.

USING INFORMAL ASSESSMENTS TO GUIDE INSTRUCTION

Assessment tells teachers what students are learning, whether they are progressing, and which aspects of the instructional program have been internalized. Informal assessments are the ongoing measures that guide teachers to adjust instruction in order to better ensure student learning.

What happens if informal assessments are not used in the classroom and instruction is not based on what students know and need to learn? Assessment practices may over-rely on standardized tests that come at the end of the year, too late to identify students' learning needs and help them progress. The curriculum may be delivered in a uniform manner and be inaccessible to certain groups of learners.

If teachers do not use informal assessments to regularly check for understanding and monitor student progress, they may assume that all students are being equally successful in class. English learners often do their best to not stand out in class, and they will look attentive and follow classroom behavior norms even when they are not able to keep up with the stream of spoken or written language. Students may "fall through the cracks" as they are pushed along with the flow of the grade-level curriculum. Students may use coping skills to keep up and sacrifice true understanding if the classroom context does not support speaking up when help is needed.

FINDING SUPPORT THROUGH COLLABORATION

The professional knowledge and behaviors required to teach *all* students to read and write English are wide-ranging and comprehensive. When viewed as a "to-do" list, it seems practically out of reach. Here are two ideas teachers may find comforting as they work to transform all classrooms into language-enriched multilingual learning communities.

1. This task does not fall on individual classroom teachers alone. It is incumbent on schools, districts, communities, teacher education programs, and larger governing bodies to provide the procedures and resources that support teachers as they grow in this knowledge. Schools and districts can establish structures for teacher professional development, parent involvement, ongoing assessment, analysis of language demands within the curriculum, and so on, to support all school personnel in becoming more knowledgeable and effective. Teachers also have power in this process. They can garner support and collaborate with fellow teachers and support personnel in many different ways.

2. Teachers have many partners at school. Depending on each teacher's particular context, collaboration might be possible in grade-level teams, with specialist teachers such as reading specialists or ELL/ English language development teachers, or with local university practicum students. In addition, when the families and communities of students are viewed as contributors to the learning environment, as described earlier in this chapter, they are more likely to engage within classrooms. This engagement with families helps broaden the sense of ownership for student success. Finally, creating a learning community in which each student feels he or she belongs and has responsibility, goes a long way toward distributing the weight off teachers' shoulders and onto each individual in the group. Students in a classroom community learn to partner, pair up, or peer tutor. In

this way, each student is viewed as a co-teacher who supports the learning of all students in the class (Au, 2009).

Districts across the country are furthering their understanding of collaboration among general education and English language learner specialists to differentiate, and provide the best instruction for, the range of students within a classroom. One district that I frequently visit has created a collaboration rubric for assessment and staff development that includes school-level factors and instructional-level factors (Saint Paul Public Schools, 2010). School-level factors include time, space, resources, classroom placement, and professional development for collaboration. Instructional-level factors include planning, co-teaching, assessment/evaluation, and reflection. In a recent study of effective teachers of English learners, I found that collaboration with other professionals was a consistent component of the highest performing general education teachers. One teacher described her collaboration with an ELL teacher as follows: "It makes my teaching worthwhile to have her" (Helman, Magnuson, & Marx, 2008). Throughout this book you will find examples of teachers collaborating in a number of innovative ways.

SUMMARY

This chapter has set the context of increasingly diverse elementary school classrooms where students who come from many language backgrounds are learning to read and write English at the same time that they're learning to speak it. I shared tensions among the kinds of programs students currently participate in, and the professional knowledge and skills needed to create engaging multilingual learning communities that more effectively teach all students to read and write. In subsequent chapters of this book you will find in-depth descriptions of the essential knowledge and skills outlined here, along with student samples and illustrative teaching practices.

CHAPTER 2

Creating a Multilingual Classroom Community

CARRIE ENVISIONS her classroom as a community of learners who work together, support one another, and actively engage with the academic content. She believes that when students participate and engage in class, they internalize what they are learning. Carrie knows that how she organizes and manages her classroom will have a profound impact on the way students interact together. She wonders whether it is possible to bridge the great variety of experiences and backgrounds that students bring to her third-grade classroom. Students in her class speak six different languages and have a wide spectrum of out-of-school background knowledge. Each student brings to the school setting academic skills as well as cultural norms for interaction. Carrie is evaluated each year on creating a learning environment that supports positive social interaction and is adapted to students with diverse backgrounds (Minnesota Board of Teaching, 2009). How will she know whether she is succeeding in these goals?

This chapter focuses on how teachers can organize their classroom environment to be language-learning communities and tailor their instruction to improve the literacy learning of their multilingual and monolingual students. In this chapter I share research and best practices for helping diverse learners feel included and listened to, as well as allowing them to participate socially and academically. First I outline the teacher's role in organizing and managing the classroom community, and I describe procedures and activities that build a sense of community. Next I discuss school-wide structures that support parent involvement and engender a welcoming environment for students and their families. In the second half of this chapter I address ways that educators can develop two-way relationships with families to learn from and find support in the culturally and linguistically diverse communities within their schools.

SETTING UP A CLASSROOM COMMUNITY

Most U.S. states have a set of teaching standards that include the expectation for creating effective and engaging environments for all students. For example, the state of California expects teachers to "establish a climate that promotes fairness and respect" and promotes collaboration and group responsibility (California Department of Education, 1997, p. 8). Many ingredients go into structuring a welcoming and productive learning environment for all students: the physical setting, the use of clear and consistent classroom routines and procedures, a climate of acceptance and respect, and a commitment to building relationships and a collaborative spirit within the group. Here are some suggestions that can help lay the foundation for creating a multilingual classroom community.

The Physical Environment

As you look around your classroom, think about ways that it facilitates or discourages positive classroom interactions and student learning. Ask yourself some of the following questions:

- Do table or desk arrangements allow for students to comfortably work in collaborative groups?
- Is there a space for the group to come together for a classroom meeting?
- Are classroom materials, books, and technology accessible to all students?
- Are books on tape or computers available for students who could profit from multiple opportunities to hear the material?
- Are age-appropriate reference materials such as alphabets, sound charts, dictionaries, and other resource materials close at hand for students as they work?

- Are print materials available to students, such as books, magazines, dictionaries, encyclopedias, atlases, student-authored books, thematic books, leveled readers, or newspapers?
- Is there evidence of multilingualism in the classroom, such as books, alphabets, or posters in languages other than English?
- Do furnishings support reading, writing, listening, and speaking independently or in groups?
- Do students have access to writing surfaces such as paper, blank books, slates, whiteboards, and so on?
- Do literacy tools and products in the classroom resemble those used for authentic purposes outside of the classroom?
- Is there evidence of multiculturalism in the classroom, such as literacy tools and products that resemble those used by nonmajority cultures present in the classroom community? Are people of many races and ethnic origins visible on posters, books, and materials?

These questions highlight some of the ways that the physical environment of the classroom can be used to influence language and literacy engagement as well as to develop a safe, productive, and cooperative learning environment (Wolfersberger, Reutzel, Sudweeks, & Fawson, 2004).

Clear and Consistent Classroom Routines and Procedures

In order to create a sense of security and calmness in the classroom, it is important that students understand the expectations for behavior and participation. Often it is helpful for students to take part in creating a set of class rules during a group meeting. The act of sharing everyone's hopes for what classroom life will be like begins a process of community building that may be cemented day by day over the course of the school year. Quieter students may find it helpful to add their comments in small-group discussions. In some schools there is a common set of behavior expectations that are expressed in school-wide rules that are posted and reinforced throughout the building. Other schools participate in shared programs that use consistent language and social development activities such as Responsive Classroom (Northeast Foundation for Children, 2011) or PeaceBuilders (PeacePartners, 2011). Whether you develop your guidelines within the classroom or use a common set in the school, it is important that you make sure your students understand what the expected behaviors look like in action. Students should be encouraged to help one another, give positive feedback, and take initiative or responsibility. Teachers can compliment students when they see positive behaviors in action. Most important, it should be made clear that there is no tolerance for disrespect, violence, or put-downs of any kind within the learning community.

A pedagogical approach that takes into account culturally responsive classroom management practices is described by Weinstein, Curran, and Tomlinson-Clarke (2003). The authors encourage teachers to:

- Begin with an awareness of our own beliefs, biases, and assumptions about human behavior and acknowledge that differences exist among people.
- Understand that schools often perpetuate the discriminatory practices of society at large.
- Design a classroom environment that promotes positive interaction and community building.
- Establish, model, and practice norms for classroom behaviors.
- Learn to communicate with students in culturally appropriate ways.
- Work to build caring and inclusive classrooms where bullying or teasing is not permitted.
- Communicate and collaborate with families, being sensitive to differences in cultural values and communication styles.
- When behavior management issues arise, examine the ways that race and ethnicity may influence the use of disciplinary consequences.

In addition to establishing consistent guidelines for classroom behavior, it is helpful for all students, and especially English learners, to have posted procedures for the most common routines that take place in class. For example, a procedure chart might outline what to do when you want to use the restroom, sharpen a pencil, or check out a library book. A procedure chart could let students know how to get ready for the class morning meeting, participate in author's chair, or engage in a book club discussion. Once procedures are listed, they can be reviewed, practiced, and referenced as needed in the classroom. Procedure charts also can include graphics or photographs to make them easier to understand. On a recent trip to Mrs. H's class in a highly diverse, urban school, I observed that when the class was told it was time for writer's workshop, five English-learning students immediately got up to review the procedure chart that outlined steps to guide the activity. Having concrete directions to reference and follow made the students feel more secure.

A Climate of Acceptance and Respect

Along with setting, modeling, and reinforcing clear behavior expectations in the classroom comes the need to develop an atmosphere of caring. Everyone in a learning community—teachers, students, and support staff—will enjoy coming to school more if they feel appreciated. There are many ways for teachers to show students that they are valued members of the community, including greeting them at the door, using their names, asking about family members, or expressing an interest in their home languages and cultures. Encouraging students to share stories or out-of-school experiences also helps everyone in the classroom come to know and accept the personal strengths of group members. In order to promote children's positive self-esteem and support their ability to learn classroom content at the same time they're learning to speak English, it is important that we respect and accept students' use of their home languages in the classroom. Whether the differences among members of the learning community have to do with language, culture, religion, academic ability, or some other characteristic, the classroom community must have a mindset that diversity makes the group stronger. Learning a new language or a new way to play ball is interesting and exciting.

At times in classrooms, especially before respectful procedures have been fully adopted, there may be incidents of disrespect or "humor" that poke fun at a student's difference. If this behavior is left alone, it will grow and cut the roots out from under the classroom community that is being built. Although it may be difficult to confront teasing or put-downs, it is the teacher's responsibility to make sure that words and behaviors that belittle classroom members are not tolerated. Some teachers bring these incidents up in class meetings so the group can reflect on them together. Teachers who notice students laughing about others' clothing, pronunciation, lunches, and so on, take the time to stop whatever is going on and seriously discuss the issue. They know that the behavior will not stop if it is ignored.

Positive actions that teachers can take include posting artifacts relating to students' backgrounds and interests, encouraging students to help one another and work together, modeling how to be appreciative and give compliments, and helping students stand up to bullying and get help from an adult when needed. A climate of acceptance and respect helps the classroom become a safe haven to nourish everyone's wellbeing.

A Commitment to Building Relationships and a Collaborative Spirit

Relationships are key to setting up a strong classroom community, and good teacher–student relationships are integral to effective classroom management (Marzano, Marzano, & Pickering, 2003). Figure 2.1 outlines some of the ways that student-to-student and student-to-teacher bonds can be fortified through common practices both in and outside of the classroom.

SCHOOL-WIDE STRUCTURES THAT SUPPORT A WELCOMING ENVIRONMENT

In her book *Literacy in the Welcoming Classroom*, JoBeth Allen (2010) challenges educators to look at our schools from the perspective of students' families. Does the school seem to value the diverse language and background experiences of families by displaying cultural artifacts, world maps, or translated posters and directions (see Figure 2.2)? Are community liaisons available to greet and interpret when families need to solve problems at school? In what ways is input from family members sought out and used to enhance student learning?

FIGURE 2.1. Building Relationships in a Classroom Community

Teacher-to-Student	Student-to-Student
Greet students as they enter class or when you see them outside of school	Learn each classmate's name
Ask about students' families and out-of-school experiences	Work in mixed small groups throughout the day
Hold high expectations for each student	Work on collaborative or team projects
Treat each student equitably	Teach one another words and customs from each person's heritage
Show a positive and caring attitude in words and body language	Participate in partner reading or book clubs
Make a point of conferencing privately with a few students each day	Listen to one another's writing and give positive feedback
Work persistently with students who do not learn the first time to help them succeed	Play word study or other learning games with partners
Make family visits to become better acquainted	Take on classroom chores in a partnership
Attend extracurricular events in students' lives	Learn about one another with a "person of the day" activity
Share the people and experiences from your life outside of school	Share affirmations about classmates when they do something caring

Many of the ideas Allen describes for setting up a positive classroom community extend to the school at large.

- The physical environment of the school can encourage or discourage family engagement depending on whether families feel at ease there.
- Signs and materials in multiple languages and pictures of diverse people help demonstrate that the school is inclusive and welcomes everyone.
- A common set of behavior expectations gives the school a feeling of order and safety.
- Welcome signs and visual directions help families navigate school offices as they meet up with children, attend school events, and get their questions answered.

FIGURE 2.2. Displaying Cultural Artifacts That Reflect Student Diversity

- Greeting families with friendly faces and an eagerness to listen builds relationships, which are the key to forging strong bonds between families and school personnel that will enhance student learning.

Research on parent involvement in schools suggests a three-stage process of "joining." First, parents are welcomed into the school. Next, the school honors their participation. Finally, parents and schools connect with a focus on children and their learning (Mapp, 2003). In Figure 2.3, you will find several examples of these three steps.

One big idea that provides opportunities for schools to welcome, honor, and connect around children with families is to set up a family center (Henderson, Mapp, Johnson, & Davies, 2007). A family center is a place within the school where families and staff can form relationships and work together. Family centers can sponsor events such as those listed above or be a source of information for families.

As your school evaluates how to become even more welcoming, you might consider a self-assessment process such as a "Family-Friendly Checklist" (Henderson et al., 2007). The checklist is a rating scale that you can use to note your school's strengths and areas for growth in a variety of aspects of family inclusion. The various areas might include how well your school welcomes families and visitors, the openness and accessibil-

FIGURE 2.3. Steps for Encouraging Parent Participation in the School Community

Welcome	Call parents at home to welcome them to the school year
	Set up parent breakfasts or after-school "teas"
	Provide a pleasant school atmosphere for interaction
	Send multiple invitations to events
	Send positive notes about students
	Invite the whole family to attend school events or set up special events such as Grandparents Day
Honor	Show parents that their input is valued and counted on for governance of the school
	Survey parents who are not able to get to school
	Provide translation for parent notes and meetings
	Request ideas from parents and then use those ideas
	Hold meetings at times that work for families and provide childcare
	Provide opportunities for parents to participate in small-group discussions
	Learn about families—their backgrounds, languages, challenges, strengths, and interests
Connect around children	Focus on student learning in interactions with families
	Create and work on common goals
	Offer workshops that parents want such as helping your child in reading, how to help with homework, learning English, or parenting skills
	Schedule family visits to share information about each child and ideas for making the most of school
	Use family journals to communicate between home and school
	Establish home–school reading programs that send books home for evening reading

ity of the school environment and staff, and how you solicit parent input and create collaborative projects among families and school personnel. Take the time to think about and observe the school's strengths and needs in terms of providing a welcoming physical environment, staff friendliness in family interactions, resources and programs offered to families, language and cultural support, and involving parents in school decision making. You can keep a list of what your school does well already, and what next steps you might implement.

BUILDING ON THE LANGUAGES AND EXPERIENCES OF FAMILIES AND COMMUNITIES

> To let her have a time of reading and writing which is at our home and that is the one thing that is helping her get better. When she comes home from school to do homework she prepares to learn more before she plays.
>
> —*Father of a second-grade Somali student*

Families play a critical role in student literacy success in a number of ways (see Figure 2.4). Families provide the language support that will serve as

FIGURE 2.4. Families Support Children's Literacy and Language Learning

a foundation for literacy skills, and they offer the responsiveness and scaffolding that have been shown to help children self-regulate and grow in cognition (Landry & Smith, 2006). As children grow, families model and engage in literate activities together, and they support students' school learning to the best of their abilities. Still, educators often lament about how families do not do enough to support the school's literacy program. It is important to respond to these "if only parents would . . ." views about family participation (Miller, 2010).

A family can structure time and space to reinforce children's learning at home in numerous ways. In this section, I add the voices of immigrant parents to provide a better understanding of how teachers might connect classroom instruction to the languages and cultures of families and communities, and I share ideas for developing partnerships and two-way flows of information. On the one hand, teachers can communicate school information to families through family literacy nights and similar school events, through translating classroom newsletters into a variety of languages spoken by students' families, and by making parent–teacher conferences accessible to parents with limited or no English-speaking abilities. On the other hand, teachers can use families and communities as a resource for developing culturally relevant instructional practices by visiting the homes and community events of their students, recruiting the help of a community liaison to interpret parents' ideas about schooling, researching students' languages and literacy practices to better understand their specific reading and writing behaviors, and learning about the diverse cultural values and experiences of students.

FIGURE 2.5. Learning from Families

School-Based Activities	Home- or Community-Based Activities
Invite parents into the classroom for a beginning-of-the-school-year chat. This also can be arranged in small groups.*	Visit families at their home to share your hopes and plans for the student and listen to families' hopes and concerns as well (Allen, 2010).
Have students draw or write stories about family life and family members.	Send home written materials containing meaningful questions for families and students to answer together and share the answers at school. Ask families to share how they use reading or writing at home and to describe some of the important activities in their lives.
Invite parents in to share their talents such as artistry, music, or job skills.*	Take a class field trip to the neighborhoods of class members. If possible, meet up with family members to have them help guide the tour.
Hold special events for particular family members such as moms, dads, or grandparents. Have children share their schoolwork, but also make time for students to learn from their family members.*	After finding out about students' out-of-school interests, arrange to attend an event in which one or more of your students will be participating (e.g., soccer game, music performance, or family get-together). Introduce yourself and connect with families at the event.**
Ask students to bring in an artifact from home that will help the class learn more about them and their families.	Ask family leaders with whom you have connected to serve as mentors for new families (Kugler, 2011).

* Provide an interpreter as needed for families that don't speak English.

** If you don't speak the family's home language, just communicate as best you can.

Learning from Families

> It's very important that See Sing knows both Hmong and English. This is important because when she grows up she can help translate, help the community, and help the people who don't understand English that much.
>
> —*Mother of a third-grade Hmong student*

All parents want the best for their children at school. When teachers come to understand the family's goals for students, it helps us increase student motivation and bring families into our goal-setting processes. See Sing's family (all names are pseudonyms) wants her to develop bilingual language skills so that she can help her community in the future. Knowing this, a teacher might plan for ways to support the family's goal, such as complimenting her on her bilingual skills, encouraging her to write bilingual messages, or discussing opportunities for bilingual graduates in the work world. Figure 2.5 describes some of the ways teachers might learn more about their classroom families.

Sharing Information from School in Meaningful Ways

It is hard for us to communicate with the teacher....The only time we can speak to a teacher in Hmong is at conferences. It would be better if we could talk to the teachers more often. A few times the teacher tried to call home, but we couldn't communicate, so the teacher just hung up.

—*Father of a third-grade Hmong student*

Families are interested in supporting their children's success at school, and they are most likely to participate in school-based activities when they are welcomed, honored, and focused on children's learning (Mapp, 2003). In what ways might Carrie, the third-grade teacher spotlighted in this book, help her school plan valuable opportunities to engage with parents to help students succeed? Figure 2.6 outlines some traditional methods that schools use to communicate with parents and also shows how these standard formats might be adjusted to increase family involvement.

Many schools or districts rely on community liaison staff members to mediate questions and concerns between families and the school. Often families get to know their community liaison and find it easier to contact him or her to get information. Schools can build on those relationships by bringing in community liaison staff to help them plan culturally appropriate events at the right times and places and in a style that will be most appreciated by families. Translators, interpreters, classroom assistants, and community liaisons can be great sources of information about students and their families, and the knowledge they bring can be shared to enlighten educators who don't belong to the same cultural or linguistic groups. Following a brief question and answer session with a community liaison staff member, one experienced teacher stated, "After listening to the success coaches [community liaisons] I think I understand more about where the families of my English learners are coming, this will make it easier to know how to communicate with them" (Helman & Coffino, 2010).

Language and Literacy Activities That Connect to Family Experiences

Always at school they are learning something, but they are not communicating to the home to do that and that. We used to ask the children, what did you learn today? I would suggest from the school if there was a little direction to say what to do at home. If they gave us more work to do at home I think it would be better....I think they should have to say, "This is what I learned today"...then I could learn better.

—*Father of a second-grade Somali student*

In this final section, I describe some examples of activities that build on what students bring with them to the classroom—their languages, home literacy practices, and cultural values. When students sense a connection or alignment across home and school expectations, they understand more

FIGURE 2.6. Methods and Suggestions for Communicating with Parents

Family Involvement Strategy ⟶	Culturally Responsive Enhancements
Back-to-school night or Open House Take the time to listen to families before giving them a presentation.	Consider inviting parents in small groups and using the time to have them share their questions and ideas.*
Family literacy nights	Learn about how families in your school community use literacy in important ways. Show families how they can build on these practices to support the school literacy program.*
School or classroom update notes	Ensure that families receive notes that are translated into their home languages. Use photos to enhance accessibility.
Notes or calls to individual families	Focus on positive behaviors and concrete ways to work together. Share specific examples of how families are helping students learn.*
Parent committee meetings	Hold meetings at times or in off-campus locations that are accessible to more families. Share power so that families feel valued and their efforts lead to worthwhile academic progress.*

*Provide an interpreter as needed for families that don't speak English.

clearly what success looks like and why it is important. When teachers use what students already know as a launching pad for learning standards-based grade-level content, instruction makes more sense for students and achievement seems more promising to families, educators, and students.

In Elementary Classrooms:

- Send packets of at-home activities with students so they can show their parents what they are learning at school and do the activities cooperatively at home. Examples might include word or picture sorts, a book the child can read, or a journal that helps teacher and family share information.
- Find out what literacy skills students have in the home language and help them make connections across the two written language systems.
- Encourage families to develop literacy skills in the child's home language. Make sure that families know that reading books in the home language and sharing about how print works in that language are good things to do. Families also could be encouraged to compare words in the home language and English. How are the words similar or different? Our brains grow when we learn another language!

- Create a multilingual library and writing center in the classroom that features books and alphabets in many languages.
- Use photos that students have taken at home to create individual or class books about the daily activities of families. Pay special attention to describing how families use reading, writing, and storytelling as they work, play, and participate in social or religious activities.
- Invite parents into class to teach the students simple rhymes in their family's language. Find pictures to illustrate the rhymes.
- Learn to say a common phrase such as "good morning" or "friend" in multiple languages. Use the phrase in class to encourage multilingualism and community building. Write the words on a class bulletin board.
- Read multicultural literature that features students from ethnic and linguistic groups similar to those in your classroom. Look for books that discuss topics your students can relate to.
- Keep a personal picture dictionary for learning words in a new language.

In Intermediate Classrooms:

- Have an established routine for the at-home activities that students will need to do. Encourage students to review the list each day with family members and take time to discuss the content of their studies with parents in the language they understand best.
- Invite parents or community members to visit class to share their story and discuss the process of becoming bilingual.
- Participate in language clubs where students learn the basics of a new language. These classes could be scheduled before or after school or during breaks.
- Keep a chart of cognates across languages for class members to add to.

SUMMARY

Effective practices for community building in classrooms and schools involve creating a welcoming and low-stress environment with clear and positive expectations for all. There is a commitment to create strong relationships among students, families, and educators, and to collaborate on decisions. A two-way process of learning is set up between educators and the families they serve, and classroom activities are designed to honor the role that families play in children's education. With these principles in hand, and an acceptance that all children bring skills, talents, and cultural and linguistic resources to the classroom, the foundation for a multilingual classroom community is in place.

CHAPTER 3

Supporting English Language Development

Lᴀɴɢᴜᴀɢᴇ ɪꜱ so simple in many ways. Most of us learn a first language without conscious instruction and use it without thinking as we go about our daily lives. We interact with family, friends, and others with ease. It is only when our language skills do not work in a given situation, such as when we immerse ourselves in a setting where our primary oral language isn't used, that we become aware of the importance and limitations of oral language. So, in many ways, language operates subconsciously for those of us who use our home language at work, at school, and in our day-to-day lives.

For people who live multilingual lives, language takes on a more complicated, conscious role. Most likely, a multilingual speaker uses one language at home with family and another language at work or school. Multilingual people may have greater or lesser proficiency in speaking, reading, writing, or listening in one language or the other, or they may have particular strengths based on the vocabulary and language structures frequently used with each language. The fact that many of the students currently entering elementary schools bring multilingual background experiences means that an awareness of oral language needs to take on a more conscious presence in our collective educational thoughts.

The focus of this chapter is to provide information on the important role that oral language plays in developing literacy. In the first section, I discuss why language teaching is important. *Language is personal*: It is at the heart of each person's identity and sense of competence.

- Language is complex: It consists of systems of vocabulary, grammar, sound, and cultural and pragmatic features.
- Language is foundational to literacy learning: Students may be able to sound out print using the phonics code, but they will not be able to extract meaning from text if they don't understand language at the word, sentence, or text level (Bailey & Heritage, 2008).

In the second section of this chapter, I share what linguists and policymakers suggest are important terms and concepts for teachers to know about language. I also provide a glossary of useful, easy-to-access linguistic terms that have been known to put more than one teacher to sleep during an afternoon workshop!

In the third and last section of this chapter, I consider the importance of English language development for students who have not yet reached comparability to their English-speaking peers in terms of oral and written language skills (World-Class Instructional Design and Assessment [WIDA] Consortium, 2011). I provide examples of language-enriched instruction that will benefit students as they advance in their language development in English. An in-depth look at how to purposefully structure academic language learning into reading and writing lessons may be found in Chapter 7 of this book.

WHY LANGUAGE IS IMPORTANT

Language is at the heart of how people engage with one another and how we think about ourselves. Language is personal, complex, and foundational to becoming literate.

Language Is Personal

If you have ever had someone make fun of your speech or language, this section heading needs no further explanation for you. Whether it is the pronunciation of a word, the choice of vocabulary, or saying a sentence in the "wrong" way, having our language criticized or laughed at is painful. Consider the feelings that might result when whole languages are devalued or ridiculed within the larger society. As poet Gloria Anzaldúa (1987) says, "So, if you really want to hurt me, talk badly about my language. Ethnic identity is twin skin to linguistic identity—I am my language. Until I can take pride in my language, I cannot take pride in myself" (p. 59).

The language we are born into becomes part of what makes us who we are. We associate it with people who nurtured us, with whom we identify, and who will always be a part of us. Our home language also instills in us a worldview and a way of seeing how we fit. Federico Fellini said, "A different language is a different vision of life" (Cantwell, 1993). This statement likely rings true to anyone who has found that learning a new language also involves understanding the world from a new perspective.

Because language is personal, it is a way to strengthen bonds and build relationships. When educators acknowledge and validate their students' language resources, students become more confident and empowered. Instead of feeling "out of the loop," students and their families feel connected and understood. As discussed in Chapter 2, demonstrating a respect for the languages of students' families increases active involvement of everyone at school.

Language Is Complex

When we use language with others, many parallel systems work together. We simultaneously coordinate words (vocabulary) into sentences (syntax) and express them as sounds (articulation). We use what we know about the culture of the setting and people (pragmatics) to communicate in the most appropriate way. These multiple layers make language learning complicated. Imagine a time when you observed a group of people who were more expert in a field than you. They probably used words you didn't understand, and most likely their conversations were difficult to follow. Students may feel the same way in classrooms where the language is over their heads.

Researchers and teachers who study language learning note that there is a big difference between the language that we use when we interact socially and the language we use in academic settings or written texts. Figure 3.1 presents these differences.

Because learning takes place through academic language, teachers need to guide students to experience not only the content of their subject matter, but also the language with which it is learned.

Language Is Foundational to Literacy

For native English speakers and English learners alike, oral language plays a crucial role in learning to read and write (Lesaux & Geva, 2006; Snow, Burns, & Griffin, 1998). In order to comprehend or produce meaningful texts, students must understand individual words and sentence meaning, and apply their background knowledge to the text as a whole (Bernhardt, 2000). Research in the area of reading shows a strong relationship between oral language skills and later reading comprehension (Foorman & Connor, 2011). If students do not have the vocabulary and syntax or cannot decipher complex academic text structures, they will learn to decode, but they will not understand the meaning of the texts they are

FIGURE 3.1. Comparison of Interpersonal Communication and Academic Language

	Interpersonal Communication	Language of Academic Text
Primary modes of communication	Verbal and nonverbal (e.g., eye contact, hand gestures)	Written and verbal
Context of use	Used by children on the playground, in the lunch room, on the school bus, at parties, playing sports, and talking on the telephone	Used by children only in academic settings (e.g., information is read from a textbook or presented by the teacher)
Audience	Used with immediate audience, interactive	Created for distant audiences of listeners/readers who are possibly not familiar with the topic (Zwiers, 2008)
Time for ELLs to acquire facility	1–3 years	5–7 years (Cummins, 1979)
Supports for understanding	Supported by meaningful interpersonal and situational cues outside of language	Decontextualized; language is abstract
Vocabulary usage	General, contextualized words, frequent repetition of words, use of slang	General, specific, and technical words; multiple-meaning words and phrases; greater variety and sophistication of words; nuances and shades of meaning (WIDA Consortium, 2011)
Language structures	Simple, common grammatical structures; may start sentences with *and* or *but*; may not be "correct" grammar	Variety of grammatical structures and sentence complexity; common use of discourse connectors such as *first, however, nevertheless*
Discourse complexity	Less dense and specific; contains one-word and short phrases, incomplete sentences; frequent use of active voice	Large amounts of dense texts; variety of organizational types (e.g., narration, exposition, description); frequent use of passive voice

reading. Similarly, if students do not have a range of words or the ability to structure sentences, they will be unable to produce meaningful writing in English. Oral language is the foundation for both of these literacy processes.

WHAT TEACHERS NEED TO KNOW ABOUT LANGUAGE

As more students enter U.S. schools with languages other than English, it is becoming clear to policymakers, teacher educators, and credentialing organizations that expanded teaching skills are needed in order to best serve all students. Achievement gaps in reading between students from English-only and English-learner backgrounds accentuate the point that not all groups of students are meeting state benchmarks in equal measure. For this reason, teaching standards are defining more explicitly the skills and knowledge that teachers should have in order to understand language development, language diversity, and linguistic concepts that will guide their work with English learners. For example, the New York State Teaching Standards (2011) mandate that "teachers demonstrate knowledge of current research in learning and language acquisition theories and processes," and that "teachers design lesson plans and adjust instruction to include a variety of strategies that support the language acquisition needs of each student." A performance-based teacher licensing exam currently being piloted across the country rates teacher candidates on their ability to "identify the language demands of learning tasks and assessments relative to the students' current levels of academic language proficiency" (Performance Assessment for California Teachers, 2010).

In the following lists, I present a range of knowledge that researchers and linguists in the field of education have proposed as essential for teachers who work in linguistically and culturally diverse settings (Fillmore & Snow, 2002; Trumbull & Farr, 2005). These lists are followed by a glossary (Figure 3.2) that provides a helpful reference to define some of the terms that are used.

What Teachers Need to Know About Language at a Societal Level:

- Every language has its own rules for use and its own community of speakers.
- The sounds, grammar, and lexicon of standard and nonstandard dialects of English vary and may be analyzed.
- Individuals may speak more than one language or dialect without detriment to the others.
- English learners need specific conditions to improve—for example, language models, explicit instruction, feedback, and opportunities to practice.

What Teachers Need to Know About Language at an Individual Level:

- A first language typically develops as a psychosocial process.
- Second language learning is a more conscious and complex process that involves cognition, social interaction, cross-linguistic transfer, and more.

What Teachers Need to Know About Language at the Sentence and Text Level:

- Syntax varies by language system, and students may be confused by structures that are new to them.

FIGURE 3.2. Glossary of Linguistic Terms

Term	Meaning	Example
academic language	The forms and functions of language found in academic settings and text	A science textbook or piece of literature
affix	A prefix or suffix attached to a base word, root, or stem	**pre**view, tire**less**
base	A word to which affixes may be attached	**garden**er
cognate	Words that have similar spellings and meanings across languages	*radio* and *radio* (Spanish/English), *park* and *parc* (English/French)
cross-linguistic transfer	Applying what is known in one language to another language	M, S, and L have the same sounds in English and Spanish
dialect	A language variety shared by a group of people from a certain culture or region	Hispanic English, Standard American English
grapheme	The letter or letters that represent sounds in a given language	In English S represents the sound /s/, Ch represents the sound /ch/
lexicon	The collection of words in a given language, field, or person; its vocabulary	*shutter, lens,* and *aperture* are in the lexicon of photography
morpheme	The smallest unit of meaning in a word	*un, re, tract,* and *able* in *unretractable*
morpho-phonemic	Related to both meaning and sound	*sign* *signal* *resignation*
narrative text structure	The framework that underlies a story of fictional or nonfictional events	introduction, problem, resolution
orthography	The way words are structured in a language	The English spelling system
phoneme	The smallest unit of sound in a word	/p/, /o/, or /t/ in "pot"
syntax	How words are put together to form sentences in a language	The students + had + a day + off.
word root	Word parts (often Greek or Latin) that are combined to form words	trans + port = *transport*

- Academic language differs from interpersonal language in specific ways.
- Students bring culturally based narrative text structures that may differ from those in school texts.
- The grammar of word roles, their possible positioning, and the effect on meaning vary across cultures and thus may not feel "natural" to English learners.
- English learners need feedback on the structural features of written language.

- Well-written texts with a natural flow serve as good models for academic writing.

What Teachers Need to Know About Language at the Word Level:

- Words may be analyzed at the level of phonemes or morphemes.
- Not all languages have the same phonemes.
- Phonemes that are distinct across languages may cause confusion for English learners in spelling and pronunciation.
- English is an alphabetic writing system that is based on phoneme-grapheme mapping.
- Morphemes are combined in particular ways in English, and these may differ from students' home languages.
- Students learning a language may produce ungrammatical word forms for irregular words, much as native speakers do when they are learning a language.
- English words are composed of roots, bases, and affixes that influence meaning.
- Cognates are a tool for helping students understand related words or affixes across languages.
- Vocabulary is key to language and literacy development and requires focused, coherent instruction.
- English orthography is morphophonemic, that is, spelling is based on sounds, patterns, and meanings.

EFFECTIVE ENGLISH LANGUAGE DEVELOPMENT

An emerging body of research describes the importance of English language development (ELD) and gives us direction on how it might be best structured and carried out. There is a growing consensus that the language students need for school success has specific academic characteristics and will not be "picked up" simply by sitting in an English-speaking classroom. Language-enriched instruction is needed throughout the day, in both language arts and content- area lessons, as well as in "navigational" activities such as when teachers provide directions and manage transitions (Bailey & Heritage, 2008). In addition, students who are developing oral proficiency need explicit learning opportunities with the vocabulary, syntax, grammar, functions, and conventions of English, and they should be given opportunities to interact with others while using their learning (Saunders & Goldenberg, 2010).

Recommendations

Several leaders in the field of ELD instruction consolidated a list of recommendations based on the research (August, Goldenberg, Saunders, & Dressler, 2010). They advocate for:

1. Providing regular ELD instruction—some is better than none
2. Implementing a daily block of dedicated ELD instruction, even in classrooms where students are receiving their instruction in English
3. Teaching a variety of elements of English, including vocabulary, grammar, syntax, and conventions
4. Emphasizing listening and speaking, although teachers may incorporate reading and writing as well
5. Integrating meaning and communication as language structures are explicitly taught
6. Focusing on academic language as well as conversational language
7. Providing students with corrective feedback on form
8. Using English during ELD time
9. Including language-learning strategies that evolve as language skills progress
10. Having specific language objectives in mind while planning and implementing lessons
11. Maintaining ELD instruction until students are at, or close to, a level comparable to their native-English-speaking peers
12. Grouping English learners by language proficiency for ELD instruction but not segregating them by language
13. Making sure that interactive lesson components are carefully planned and implemented so they support language proficiency goals

This list of guidelines for instruction provides a roadmap for working with colleagues and school and district leadership teams to envision how English language development might be structured in each school site. There is a greater chance for successful implementation of a rigorous, coherent ELD plan when schools and districts designate it as a priority (Saunders & Goldenberg, 2010).

Organization

The kind of organizational plan for English language development instruction your school designs will vary depending on your population of students at various proficiency levels in English. Some schools and classrooms have a handful of students who have yet to achieve advanced proficiency in oral English, while other classrooms are made up almost fully of English learners at various levels of proficiency development. Discussions about providing tailored language instruction for ELL students are most effective at the school level because resources are needed to help teachers learn about and carry out lessons at students' language levels. Often, setting up rigorous and ongoing ELD instruction will require teamwork between the classroom teacher and school ELL support teacher.

At Carrie's school, only students at the early levels of English language development (entering and beginning levels) receive any structured ELD lessons with the grade-level ELL support teacher, Anne. Carrie feels lucky to work with Anne, who spends 30 minutes a day in Carrie's classroom to support the 10 English learners at the earliest levels of English proficiency. Since Anne has a background in language development and ELD instruction, she not only provides differentiated small-group instruction to Carrie's students at the entering and beginning levels, but also is able to provide advice to Carrie about how her teaching could be made more understandable for students learning English. The two teachers meet one afternoon a week to plan together for ELD goals and upcoming lessons. They have found that collaboration improves their work with students because they can exchange their perspectives and expertise and make connections between ELD and core classroom instruction (Honigsfeld & Dove, 2010).

While Anne is in Carrie's classroom, she spends 15 minutes with each of the two ELD groups. She plans a lesson specific to her district's ELD standards for each group. While she is working with one group, the other group is participating in an interaction activity that is based on students' oral proficiency level. The entering-level group may be listening to a simple text on tape, or students may be playing a vocabulary game with a partner. The beginning-level group may be reading in pairs and discussing a story, or reviewing language strategies from the previous day's lesson. During the 30-minute ELD block, Carrie manages two groups as well: one group of English learners who are further along on the proficiency continuum, and another group of students who are native English speakers. She plans and works directly with the ELL students and sets up activities for her native English speakers that provide language enrichment. When possible, Carrie finds university students or community volunteers to come in and support the language activities during this time of the school day.

Figure 3.3 provides a brief overview of the organization of Carrie's 30-minute ELD block. She finds that the time goes at a fast pace and requires planning, but the explicit language being learned makes it very much worth the effort.

Many readers probably are wondering what options they have in implementing explicit ELD instruction if they do not have an ELL support teacher like Anne. While there are no simplistic solutions to this problem, here are some beginning ideas:

- Does your school use a pull-out model for ELD? If so, consider transforming the structure to a push-in model so that a collaborative, integrated system can be nurtured. This will help more students to be served.
- Consider planning ELD instruction in grade levels or grade-level bands of classrooms. Designate a regular time for ELD and have students attend the classroom that is geared to their proficiency level for 15–20 minutes a day.
- Involve other resource teachers, school staff, parent volunteers, and university students to help you staff your ELD instructional time.

FIGURE 3.3. A Sample ELD Block from Carrie's Classroom

	ELL Teacher's Group (Anne)	Teacher's Group (Carrie)
First 15 minutes	Anne works with students at the entering level in explicit ELD instruction for vocabulary, grammar, and syntax. Anne monitors the beginning level group as students do guided practice with previous ELD strategies.	Carrie works with students at the developing and expanding levels of proficiency on explicit language instruction such as understanding and producing more complex sentence structures. Students who do not need ELD instruction participate in language enrichment activities (e.g. thematic book clubs, independent research, or independent reading and writing).
Second 15 minutes	Anne works with students at the beginning level in explicit ELD instruction for vocabulary, grammar, and syntax. Anne monitors the entering level group as students do receptive language activities such as listening to stories on tape or practicing vocabulary with a partner.	Carrie gathers both the ELL and native English speakers in her group to listen to a read-aloud text with frequent think-pair-share questions embedded. She partners students with differing levels of English proficiency so that ELL students are integrated and have opportunities to work with an English language model.

If ELD instruction is made a priority, resources will be located to support the effort.

- Lead the conversation for ELD support at the school leadership team level. Many students are held back from meeting grade-level performance benchmarks because they are not given explicit instruction in oral and written language. Supporting ELD increases success in school-wide goals.

Sample Instruction

In the final section of this chapter, I present a few peeks into what explicit instruction in ELD might look like during the block of time that is geared specifically toward language development. These vignettes are just samples and are not meant to be inclusive of the range of excellent ELD instruction possible. For additional ideas, look at the English language development section of "Planning Instruction" in the Appendix to this book. Chapter 7 also highlights classroom instruction in reading and writing that enhances academic language development for all students.

EXAMPLE 1. A group of students at the *entering* level of English language proficiency are learning grade-level content words by reviewing pictures and other visuals (WIDA Consortium, 2011). Students practice

FIGURE 3.4. Sample Sentence Construction Chart on Magnetism

The magnet attracts _____, but it won't attract _____.

coins	metal	paper	spoons
books	wood	nails	jars
plants	plastic	cups	knives
rings	forks	screws	fingers

saying the words and following one-step commands such as, "Touch the ocean picture. Walk to the mountain picture. Point to the river picture." Students answer simple questions such as, "What do you see?" with "I see a _____."

EXAMPLE 2. Students at the *beginning* level of English language proficiency work on more general academic vocabulary and use expanded sentence constructions (WIDA Consortium, 2011). Students ask each other simple questions that include the target vocabulary. For example, a group of first-grade students is reviewing the story language of beginning, middle, and end. First, the teacher reads a simple, action-oriented story to the group. Any important vocabulary words are briefly discussed, clarified, and acted out. Next, students work with the teacher to identify what happens at the beginning, middle, and end of the story. The teacher models the following sentence patterns: "At the beginning, the _____" (e.g., girl finds a dog); "In the middle, the _____" (e.g., dog comes to her house); "At the end, the _____" (e.g., girl finds the dog's owner). The teacher provides gentle corrective feedback as students use the frame sentences. Students also practice using the following phrase with a partner, "Tell me about the _____"(e.g., beginning, middle, or end). Students respond with the frame sentence practiced earlier.

EXAMPLE 3. Students at the *developing* level of English language proficiency work on expanded general and specific academic language related to content-area studies. They work on both oral and written language (WIDA Consortium, 2011). For example, a third-grade group of students uses a frame sentence to create sentences based on their study of magnetism (Dutro & Helman, 2009). The frame sentence states, "The magnet attracts _____, but it won't attract _____." (E.g., The magnet attracts *coins*, but it won't attract *books*.) The frame sentence and vocabulary chart look something like Figure 3.4.

The teacher starts the lesson by reviewing the vocabulary words, adding pictures where needed. Next the students repeat the frame sentence as the teacher models her sentence. The students practice creating and sharing sentences, and they ask one another questions about their constructions. When the oral component of the lesson is over, students write three sentences of their own using the structure and vocabulary from the lesson.

On the following day, students will read their sentences to one another and ask more questions.

SUMMARY

These three examples demonstrate the need for differentiated ELD instruction for students at various levels of proficiency. Chapter 7 in this book expands on these ideas by describing ways to integrate vocabulary and academic language into reading and writing lessons in the classroom.

CHAPTER 4

Understanding English Learners' Reading Development

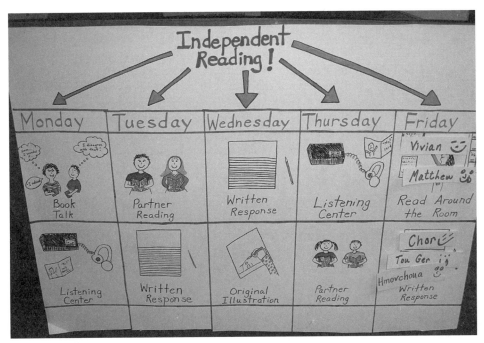

To ADAPT an old phrase: Readers are made, not born. Becoming a capable reader in English begins with our early experiences with print, whether in books, in notes, on cereal boxes, on traffic signs, or on the computer screen. During these emergent literacy experiences children join together their oral language—the words, stories, songs, and conversations of their lives—with the medium of text. The process of reading development builds on children's oral language and expands as they learn the features of print, individual sounds in spoken words (phonemic awareness), the phonetic code of written English (effortless decoding), and the importance of making meaning (comprehension) (National Reading Panel, 2000).

HOW READING DEVELOPS

The process of reading development may be described as a progression from emergent to advanced capabilities. On this path, students consolidate their decoding skills in the beginning reading phase, develop fluent and expressive pacing in the transitional phase, and build expertise in a variety of genres and reading styles in the intermediate phase (Foorman & Connor, 2011). In the following series of brief descriptions, I outline key developmental milestones at each step along the way.

Emergent Readers

Rosita is paging through a picture book in her kindergarten class, chanting the repeated phrase, "Not I, said the hen." She is able to write the letters of her name and knows eight of the letter sounds in English. Rosita is working on learning the alphabet, increasing her basic vocabulary in English, identifying individual sounds in words, and understanding themes in classroom read-aloud material.

Emergent Readers:

- Imitate reading behaviors of others
- "Pretend read" stories based on what they have memorized or imagine from picture cues
- Are developing knowledge of the alphabetic system of English
- Begin to play with sounds in oral language and may be developing phonological awareness skills such as rhyming, alliteration, and blending sounds into words

Beginning Readers

Daniel takes out his box of books as he warms up for a small-group reading lesson with his teacher. He reads three little books that have one to two sentences per page. His concentration is intense as he points to each word and says it aloud. The vocabulary is accessible, and unusual words are depicted in the illustrations, so in this task he does not struggle with comprehension. Daniel is working on consolidating his understanding of phonics in English, and re-reading simple materials so he can gain reading fluency.

Beginning Readers:

- Use their knowledge of high-frequency words and sound–symbol correlations to decode simple texts
- Develop the ability to segment oral words into their individual sounds, and point to words as they read

- Read slowly in a word-by-word manner
- Expand their knowledge of the sounds and patterns of English on a daily basis and begin to gain some fluency

Transitional Readers

Maleeah has finished her assignment and opens her well-worn beginning chapter book to the spot where she left a bookmark. The text has action, mystery, and humor, and still embeds illustrations to support her growing fluency. She can read the book in three or four sittings, although the word play and idiomatic expressions sometimes make it difficult for her to completely understand what is going on.

Transitional Readers:

- Use their expanded sight-word reading vocabulary and decoding skills to read longer texts with some fluency
- Read faster, but often lack expressiveness
- May not understand all of the words they can read and may need to be supported in strategies for self-monitoring their comprehension
- May enjoy reading series books that follow the adventures of a particular character within a familiar context

Intermediate Readers

Azeem's eyes move quickly through the words of his novel as he reads two chapters that he will soon discuss with his book group in class. His concentration is intense, and he periodically laughs or shakes his head from side to side. He wonders what others in his group will think about the events of this chapter. He thinks it will be a good group discussion!

Intermediate Readers:

- Read silently in longer texts on their own
- Have developed preferences about what materials they prefer to read for pleasure
- Read fluently and expressively
- Face challenges with vocabulary and academic language in the longer and conceptually deep materials they are reading

Advanced Readers

Jessica lugs a variety of reading materials in her backpack as she maneuvers around her high school, including science, math, and social studies textbooks, a novel for English, as well as the school newspaper. She can be spotted reading throughout the day as she catches up on her homework or her favorite current events blog, and fills a spare moment with her out-of-school book of choice.

Advanced Readers:

- Read at quick rates (i.e., frequently greater than 200 words per minute)
- Slow down when reading difficult or unfamiliar material
- Learn most new vocabulary through print
- Access a variety of reading materials throughout the day, depending on needs and preferences

READING IN A FIRST OR SECOND LANGUAGE

How is the process of learning to read different for Rosita, Daniel, and the other students described above who did not use English regularly until they arrived at elementary school? What do Carrie and the other main-stream classroom teachers need to know to help their English-learning students grow in their decoding capabilities, comprehension, and motivation for reading?

All students, whether native speakers or English learners, must learn the code of the English writing system as well as make sense of the language in order to derive meaning from text (Lesaux & Geva, 2006). Although students vary greatly in the amount of vocabulary and oral language skills they possess, most native speakers of English have a basic vocabulary that will help them understand the language of early reading materials. English learners, on the other hand, may not be familiar with even common words; thus, one essential task for Carrie's teaching will always be to ensure that students comprehend the message of the text, even for lessons that focus on a reading skill.

In Figure 4.1, I outline basic components of reading and point out how these areas may be more complex for students learning to read in English as a new language (see Helman, 2009).

ONE ENGLISH LEARNER'S READING DEVELOPMENT

Kevin and his family came to the United States from Mexico in the summer before he entered first grade. Although he was not yet reading, Kevin had been to kindergarten in Mexico and had learned some letter–sound correspondences in Spanish. He did not speak or understand English. Kevin's reading development highlights the challenges and successes of a student learning to read in a new language.

FIGURE 4.1. The Components of Reading and Their Complexities for Language Learners

Component	Basic Principles	Language Learners
Phonemic awareness	All students must first be able to discriminate individual sounds in words in order to use the alphabetic system to decode or write new words.	Phonemic awareness is facilitated when students know many words in a language. Students with limited vocabularies may have difficulty associating commonalities (such as beginning or ending sounds) across unknown words.
	With the wide range of words in their oral repertoires and their years of experience listening to and speaking these words, native speakers have easier access to distinguishing commonalities across words, such as what they sound like at the beginning, middle, or end, or whether they rhyme.	Sounds that are not present in students' home languages may be difficult for students to identify and differentiate. For example, the sounds of the short e and short i are not present in Spanish, so they are difficult for students to distinguish in oral language.
		Students who have phonemic awareness skills in a home language are able to transfer this conceptual knowledge to English.
Phonics	English is an alphabetic writing system so all students must learn how sounds are represented by letters or letter combinations.	Students who bring literacy knowledge from an alphabetic home language have the potential to transfer those skills to reading in English.
	Native speakers may have more extended experiences with printed words in English, thereby scaffolding their beginning phonics knowledge.	Students who bring literacy knowledge from a nonalphabetic home language may need explicit instruction to become aware of the alphabetic principle in written language.
		Students who have phonetically transparent home languages may find the complex spelling patterns (e.g., numerous vowel patterns) of English challenging.
Vocabulary and oral language	When students have strong vocabularies and understand complex language patterns, they are able to use this knowledge to extract meaning from text. Native-speaking children bring a subconscious understanding of how words are put together to form cohesive phrases. They also are likely to have a more extensive knowledge of word meanings to aid their understanding of texts.	Non-native speakers have fewer oral English resources to bring to the task of reading. Because they are less familiar with English syntax, they may find it difficult to predict words from context in a reading passage.
		English learners are likely to encounter many unknown words in the texts they are reading, even in beginning reading materials. In order for reading to not be reduced to mere decoding, students need ways to learn the meanings of words that are important to text comprehension.
		Students bring knowledge of words in their home language to their reading in English. When students' word knowledge includes cognates with English words (e.g., *radio* in both English and Spanish), their language resources can be enhanced.

FIGURE 4.1. Continued

Component	Basic Principles	Language Learners
Fluency	As students develop accurate and automatic decoding skills, their reading speed and expression improve. For native speakers, fluency is associated with greater comprehension in the early stages of reading development. When fluency is labored, understanding of the meaning of the text may be impaired.	Some English learners may develop what appear to be automatic decoding skills, but still may not understand what they are reading. Fluency work with English learners should include a focus on comprehension and oral language development. After vocabulary has been clarified, students profit from repeated readings of the same text.
Comprehension	Comprehension is the primary goal of the reading process for all students. Comprehension may be obstructed when students are not able to automatically and fluently decode the text, when they do not understand the meanings of words, when they do not have the background knowledge needed to make sense of the text, or when the text structures are too complex for students to decipher.	Students who are learning a new language as well as new discourse processes in their classrooms are likely to find additional roadblocks on the way to comprehension: unknown vocabulary, complex academic language structures, and distinct cultural ways of knowing and communicating. Students who bring literacy skills from a home language will likely transfer their comprehension strategies to English reading. Students who are developing literacy in their second language may need explicit instruction in applying comprehension strategies.
Motivation (Archambault, Eccles, & Vida, 2010)	Students who feel capable in their reading and writing ability are more likely to take on challenging tasks and persevere when more effort is needed, whereas a lower self-perception may lead students to give up during the literacy event. Students who are interested in and enjoy reading and writing are likely to do them more, find them more important, and, in turn, get better at them.	English learners are a diverse group of students from many background experiences and with varied cultural values. Connecting school-based literacy learning to students' home values may increase students' engagement and interest in reading and writing. Demonstrating the purpose and benefits of academic literacy tasks also may increase students' intrinsic motivation for engaging in language arts activities.

FIGURE 4.2. Kevin's Emergent Writing Sample

Emergent Reading

Kevin began his first-grade year as an emergent reader. Early in the year he was able to read about half of the words in the simplest of predictable readiness-level readers in the reading series at his school. Kevin was developing phonological skills such as identifying rhymes and beginning sounds in words. Figure 4.2 shows that Kevin's writing sample early in first grade included writing his name (removed for anonymity), the word *mom*, and the letters *llae* to represent "baby."

Much of Kevin's energy as an emergent learner was spent acquiring the English words necessary to understand and participate in activities in his classroom. During first grade, Kevin moved from Level 1 (non-English speaking) to Level 2 (limited English speaking) on a standardized measure of oral language development. Over the course of the year, Kevin learned the letters and sounds of the English alphabet, developed the phonemic awareness skills of blending and segmenting sounds in words, and began to read at an instructional level in the earliest decodable books. During first grade he had moved from being an emergent reader to a beginning reader.

Beginning Reading

Once Kevin's alphabetic, phonological, and early language skills began to come together to help him understand the phonetic code of the English writing system, Kevin began to decode early reading materials. As a beginning reader in his second-grade year, Kevin progressed from reading at a readiness level at the start of the school year to reading texts that were classified as middle of first-grade level by the end of the school year. In many ways, during his second-grade year Kevin followed the learning pattern of a typical first grader. He read and reread very simple decodable texts from September through November, and his text-level progress showed little change. Beginning in November, however, and throughout the rest of the academic year, Kevin's growth accelerated as he read increasingly complex first-grade texts. Kevin also added many high-frequency words to his reading vocabulary. In his end-of-second-grade writing sample, Kevin's increased literacy knowledge was evident as he wrote, *"When I go to the market I am happy becaus I get to die meny things"* (When I go to the market, I am happy because I get to buy many things).

Transitional Reading

Transitional readers are gaining fluency and automaticity (or the ability to do things without thinking about the low-level details required, allowing it to become an automatic response pattern or habit) in their reading and are able to read longer and more varied texts. Kevin demonstrated the qualities of a transitional reader from the middle of his third-grade year through the middle of his fourth-grade year. His ability to read longer texts, such as early chapter book adventure stories, gave him more choices and more reading practice. In fourth grade, Kevin stated that he thought he was getting better at reading and needed less help than he used to. He expressed a lack of confidence in his ability, however, when compared with other students. On a test of word reading and passage decoding that was administered at the end of fourth grade, Kevin scored at a sixth-grade level. This was higher than the text level he worked with in class, and it showed that decoding words was not a problem for him. Still, he missed several of the comprehension questions about the text because of lack of familiarity with many of the higher level, academic English vocabulary words and complex sentence structures.

Intermediate Reading

By late fourth grade and early fifth grade, Kevin's reading abilities put him at an early intermediate level. During his fifth-grade year, Kevin grew in fluency on the school's grade-level benchmark passages, scoring between 118 to 170 words correct per minute. An example of a chapter book that he chose for independent reading was *Stuart Little* (White, 1945). This book is classified as having a reading level of approximately late third grade.

Kevin was a member of a diverse classroom composed of primarily non-native speakers of English. His teacher characterized him as one of the strongest readers in the class and described the significant progress Kevin had made throughout the year. While the teacher had seen much success in the accuracy and fluency of Kevin's reading toward grade-level benchmarks, he noted that comprehension was an area where Kevin needed to focus. As a student who has reached the intermediate level, Kevin generally will not be held back by the level of his decoding skills, but rather will need to find ways to access the complex academic language of texts that he will encounter in his upcoming middle school classroom.

WHAT WE LEARN FROM KEVIN'S READING DEVELOPMENT

Each student brings many unique resources to his or her schooling experience, and Kevin represents only one of many diverse case examples for English learners attending elementary schools. Students vary in their time in the new country, previous schooling experiences, knowledge of English, background experiences, and familiarity with the school culture, to name just a few factors. Still, there are many aspects of Kevin's story that help teachers see how reading development might vary for bilingual students.

Kevin arrived in the United States at the beginning of first grade having attended school for 1 year in Mexico. Although his previous schooling was not extensive, Kevin did have some phonological skills and letter–sound awareness that likely would help him understand the code of written English. A wise teacher might assess Kevin's literacy knowledge in Spanish to see how it could be built upon to develop English literacy skills.

Kevin's learning trajectory shows progress that was at times slow and measured and at times accelerated and dramatic. As a first grader, he learned what most would consider kindergarten emergent literacy skills. As a second grader, Kevin was a solid beginning reader, typically thought of as a first-grade level, and did not develop the fluency of a transitional reader until the middle of third grade. His learning pace in first through third grades was steady, with some periods of plateau and some regression over the summer months. Kevin also showed that once he had a better understanding of the written code of English, his word recognition and fluency increased exponentially. Thus, even though Kevin began his schooling at nearly a year below grade-level expectations and seemed to lag over several years, once he began to master code-related tasks, he experienced a spurt in growth that gave him access to grade-level material.

SUMMARY

Kevin's story highlights a major concern for teachers working with language learners: Even as students learn the processes of automatic and fluent decoding of text, they struggle with comprehending the advanced vocabulary and academic language of those texts. While Kevin is on track in speed and accuracy benchmarks for his grade level at the end of fifth grade, he does not always comprehend what he reads and frequently searches for English words to express his conceptual understanding. His journey reminds educators to look deeper into the assessment processes we use to make sure that reading progress includes students' abilities to extract meaning from written texts. Following is a list of some important features of reading development that teachers will want to keep in mind as they work with their emerging English learners.

KEY IDEAS ABOUT READING DEVELOPMENT FOR ENGLISH LEARNERS (HELMAN & BEAR, 2007)

- Students bring unique language and literacy experiences with them to the classroom.
- Many reading skills can be transferred from a student's home language to English.
- Students learning English may take longer to move through the developmental levels of reading.
- Students may learn to decode texts quickly and accurately, but still not comprehend what they are reading.

Understanding English Learners' Writing Development

Using writing for purpose and pleasure is a key aspect of literacy development. From early drawings and scribbles on a page, to writing names and notes, to writing thoughts into narrative or informational pieces of text, children write to communicate, reflect, and share meaning with the world. Reading and writing are interactive processes that overlap in many ways. Students bring what they know about language, vocabulary, letters, sounds, and word patterns to both the reading and writing processes (Berninger, Cartwright, Yates, Swanson, & Abbott, 1994; Ehri, 1997). Writing is more cognitively demanding than reading, however. Most students are able to read a word or sentence much sooner than they would be able to write the same word or sentence. Because both reading and writing call on similar pools of knowledge, growth in one area tends to go hand-in-hand with growth in the other. For example, when a child develops the phonemic awareness necessary to begin decoding words based on their letter sounds, it won't be long before that same child will try spelling using sounds, as well (Read, 1971). This connection between reading and spelling has been described as a *synchrony* (Bear, Invernizzi, Templeton, & Johnston, 2012).

In this chapter, I describe the synchrony of students' writing and spelling development with their reading development. First, I give a brief overview of how spelling progresses on a developmental continuum. Next, I share developmental writing samples from an English-learning student as he progresses through the emergent, alphabetic, pattern, and morphophonemic levels of word knowledge. I point out important benchmarks to help teachers identify students' understanding of words in English and connect this back to the synchrony of their reading and writing development. I discuss, by analyzing examples of students' developmental writing, what teachers can find out about their students' language learning, word knowledge, awareness of print conventions, and development of a writer's voice. Later in the chapter I describe a variety of ways that teachers can support spelling and writing development by increasing their awareness of the sounds and story structures in their students' home languages, guiding students with text models, and integrating writing for authentic purposes in the classroom community.

THE SYNCHRONY OF READING AND SPELLING DEVELOPMENT

Figure 5.1 outlines how reading and spelling grow together as students' literacy skills evolve. This developmental model helps teachers understand the lens young students use to view the world of written language at any given point in time. As students gain insights through one mode (e.g., reading), it contributes to their understanding of the whole literacy system of a particular language. For this reason, examining students' developmental spelling and unedited writing samples provides a window into what they know about literacy in general (Henderson, 1990).

ONE ENGLISH LEARNER'S WRITING DEVELOPMENT

Abdirahman was born in a refugee camp in Kenya to a Somali family and came to the United States when he was 6 years old. He enrolled in kindergarten in February of the year that he arrived, and he has lived in the same urban midwestern city for his entire elementary school career, although he transferred from a public school to a charter school at the beginning of his fourth-grade year. Abdirahman's growth in spelling and writing over the course of 5 years demonstrates a movement from the emergent to the intermediate level. There is much to find out by investigating his progress and his challenges as an English learner developing literacy skills.

FIGURE 5.1. The Synchrony of Reading and Spelling (Bear et al., 2012)

	Reading Behaviors	**Writing/Spelling Behaviors**
Emergent reader and speller	Students pretend-read or memorize texts and read without using phonetic clues. As letter–sound knowledge and phonemic awareness develop, students begin to use phonics to identify particular words.	Students draw, scribble, or make letter-like marks. Later, students write memorized words such as names or things of importance. With increasing alphabetic and phonological skills, students begin to represent a salient sound in their spelling of a word (e.g., M for *mom*).
Beginning reader/ spelling by sound	Students decode texts using knowledge of sight words and phonics. Reading tends to be a slow, word-by-word process. With continued practice word reading becomes more automatic and some fluency develops.	Students use their developing phonemic awareness to identify and represent the individual sounds in words they write. Early alphabetic spellers may represent one sound in a word (e.g., B for *book*) while fully alphabetic spellers will represent each sound heard (e.g., BUK for *book*). Writing is a slow and labor-intensive process of sounding out individual words and attaching letters to represent those sounds.
Transitional reader/ spelling by pattern	Fluency and expression increase while reading. Students read more extended texts with a smaller proportion of illustrations. As reading pace quickens, readers come to prefer silent reading.	Students are fully alphabetic in their spelling (e.g., GARDIN for *garden*) and begin to represent long vowel and other vowel patterns in their writing (e.g., CHUED for *chewed*). Writing flows more easily and is readable, if not completely correct. Students may use prewriting activities to plan for writing more extended pieces.
Intermediate reader/ spelling by sound, pattern, and meaning	Students read fluently and expressively in longer texts. Their primary challenge comes from demands for vocabulary, academic language, and increased background knowledge.	Students spell single-syllable words correctly and are learning the guidelines for combining syllables and adding affixes to words. They begin to use morphemes—the meaningful chunks of words—to build their vocabulary and spelling skills. Students write fluently for various purposes and audiences.

Emergent Writing

Abdirahman's writing sample in the fall of first grade shows his developing skills as an emergent reader and writer. (See Figure 5.2.) He uses a mix of letters and numbers, some written in reverse. It is unclear whether he has maintained a consistent left-to-right directionality; however, he has created lines of text. When asked to tell this story, he dictated, "My self eating hamburger. I say, 'Mommy will you pick me apple?' 'Yes I can.' I pick it. I eat it. That's it. That's it."

FIGURE 5.2. Abdirahman's Emergent-Writing Sample

Abdirahman's writing and oral language dictation tell us a lot about what he is learning. He knows that text conveys the message in a story and he knows what letters look like. His story has characters, action, resolution, and even dialogue. His language shows that he can express himself in basic terms in English using the present tense, but he runs out of words to fill out his description.

Spelling by Sound

In January of his first-grade year, 3 months after the writing sample in Figure 5.2, Abdirahman shows that he has developed some good alpha-

FIGURE 5.3. Abdirahman's Early Alphabetic Writing

betic and phonological knowledge. He is able to isolate sounds in words and he can find letters to represent them as he writes, "I like to play. I like to color." (See Figure 5.3.) As is typical with students who are spelling by sound, it took him a long time to spell these sentences, so the product doesn't represent a complex or deep narrative.

Four months later, in May of his first-grade year, Abdirahman shows even greater skills in spelling by sound. He writes, "OWT ITOYM WE RE-ING DNA WE SE A MUS COM IN OR SCOOWL AND WE THEN TO THE PRG GROWAND." He read his text as: "One time we was reading and we saw a mouse come in our school and we then to the playground we went to the playground." Here, Abdirahman demonstrates excellent phonemic awareness skills. He distinguishes most of the individual sounds in words and even stretches some words out to distinguish the sounds within a diphthong such as in his spelling of *school* as SCOOWL. His syntactical skills are more advanced than in the previous sample, as he expresses the whole story in one long sentence of 20 words.

FIGURE 5.4. Abdirahman's Spelling by Pattern

Spelling by Pattern

Through most of second grade, Abdirahman continued to work at an alphabetic level of spelling, although he was able to write more with less effort. By the end of the second grade, his developmental spelling assessment showed him "using but confusing" the long vowel pattern. He correctly spelled HOPE, SHINE, and DREAM, but he wrote *blade* as BLAD and *coach* as COCH. His writing sample about going to the market is shared in Figure 5.4.

In this example Abdirahman shows that he knows plenty of sight words such as *went, own, give,* and *apple.* He uses BOUT for *bought* and LITTEL for *little.* Like other transitional readers who are learning spelling patterns, he is much more fluent in his writing and shows clear word boundaries and punctuation. His story gives us insight into his developing English skills: He uses very simple language and reverts to the present tense when he has difficulty with a past-tense construction.

In early third grade, Abdirahman is an advanced pattern speller. He correctly spells *float, train,* and *bright,* and is using but confusing other vowel patterns, such as writing SPOUL for *spoil,* SURVING for *serving,* and CHOUD for *chewed.* His writing is quick and readable and he now uses it to share ideas, take notes, and stay organized.

FIGURE 5.5. Abdirahman's Final Writing Sample

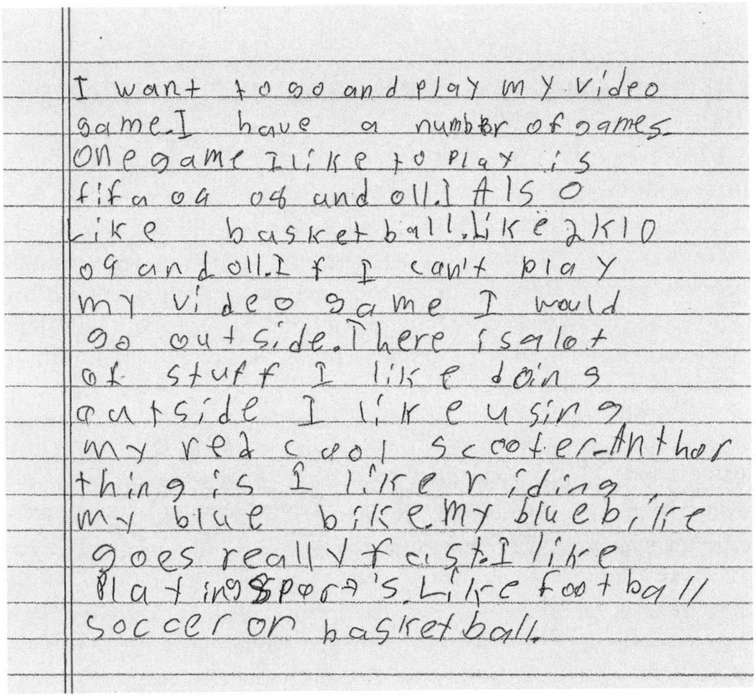

I want to go and play my video game. I have a number of games. One game I like to play is fifa 04 04 and oll. I Also like basketball. like 2k10 04 and oll. If I can't play my video game I would go outside. There is a lot of stuff I like doing outside I like using my red cool scooter. Anther thing is I like riding my blue bike. My blue bike goes really fast. I like playing Sport's Like football soccer or basketball.

Using Sound, Patterns, and Meaning to Spell Multisyllabic Words

By fourth grade Abdirahman is moving beyond the pattern stage of spelling. He correctly spells all single-syllable words from the developmental spelling inventory and is challenged by what to do when syllables join to form longer words. For example, he spells *carries* as CARRYES and *ripen* as RIPPEN. His spring writing sample has no misspelled words: "I like wolves because they are scary. And they howl at night to the moon. They run fast and have sharp teeth." Once students develop conventional spelling skills, it becomes more difficult to assess their word knowledge simply by reading their unedited writing. An advanced spelling or academic vocabulary spelling assessment could be given to pinpoint their next steps for instruction. Figure 5.5 shows Abdirahman's final writing sample from fifth grade.

He demonstrates conventional spelling skills and he has a good handle on writing conventions. Abdirahman's voice and personal interests seem to spring off the page. He is an active boy who likes to keep moving and is anxious to get his writing done quickly, too. No syntactical errors are evident in his writing, although his range of vocabulary in English is still thin in relation to the standards set for fifth graders. Abdirahman has made excellent growth in spelling and writing in synchrony with his reading development through his elementary experience. The challenges that await him in middle school involve how to rapidly expand his academic language skills and depth of vocabulary knowledge in English.

SUPPORTING ENGLISH LEARNERS' SPELLING AND WRITING DEVELOPMENT

In a multilingual classroom with each student on his or her own literacy learning path, just as Abdirahman has been, third-grade teacher Carrie wonders how she will be able to provide at just the right time what each student needs. She is clear that her whole-group lessons do not address the range of developmental needs in her classroom, but wonders whether she somehow should completely individualize her spelling and writing instruction.

Happily for Carrie and other teachers, one-on-one writing instruction is not required. There are lots of ways to support students' writing progress in small group and open-ended activities that allow everyone to work at their own level. In this section, I provide examples of multi-purpose learning activities that increase students' interest in writing and word study while providing a strong scaffold for them to develop written language skills. In the next section of this chapter, I begin by offering a few tips concerning classroom organization and planning that will facilitate your writing instruction. Next, I share some examples of how to connect writing to students' languages and experiences. Following that, I describe how to use modeling and explicit instruction to scaffold students' writing growth at the word and sentence levels. I end the chapter with many examples of how you can use writing for authentic purposes in your classroom community.

Tips for Classroom Organization

A simple first step for organizing classroom writing and word study instruction is to assess your students on a developmental spelling inventory such as the *Primary Spelling Inventory* or the *Elementary Spelling Inventory* (Bear et al., 2012). After asking your students to spell a set of words "the best they can," you can score the inventories and see what understandings your students have about the written language system in English. If you have students who speak Spanish, Korean, or Chinese, spelling inventories are also available in those languages (Helman, Bear, Templeton, Invernizzi, & Johnston, 2012). This information can help you build on the literacy knowledge that students bring from their home languages.

Once you have identified students' developmental levels, group the class into three word study groups so they can engage in material at their instructional levels. Students who are using alphabetic/sound strategies for spelling will profit from word and picture sorts, games, and activities that help them refine their phonetic understandings. Students who are ready to explore vowel patterns or multisyllabic words will grow from experiences with more complex word study. All students will benefit from opportunities to focus on words that are at the right level of challenge. Follow up on word study lessons with opportunities to read and write real texts that feature the words under study. When students are encouraged to use what they know about words and sentence structure to create their own messages, they put their new learning into practice.

Try having a range of materials around to support students' developing writing. Kindergarten through third grade students get practice composing by using a variety of materials stored in an accessible location in the classroom, such as paper, booklets, postcards, notepaper, markers, pencils and pens, whiteboards, magnet boards, simple writing software on computers or tablets, and so on. Fourth through sixth grade students engage well with journals and word study notebooks where they can put their writing notes, keep lists of important words or ideas, and reflect on their learning. Age-appropriate reference materials are also helpful to students. These might include picture dictionaries, bilingual dictionaries, alphabets, rhyming dictionaries, and web access to look up words or reference information. As discussed in Chapter 2, it is very helpful to have charts of directions, procedures, and lists of words available for students to reference in the classroom during writing activities.

Connect Writing to Students' Languages and Experiences

There are many ways to link writing to the resources that students bring with them to school. An added benefit is that writing serves as a way for teachers to learn about students' interests, families, languages, and aspirations. In Chapter 2 I described several ways to use writing to make family connections; one of those suggestions was to have students write stories about family life and family members. Journals can be sent home for students and families to use to describe the important activities in their lives or communicate information between families and teachers. Photographs of students' families and neighborhoods can be the illustrations for culturally relevant writing projects.

Socorro Herrera (2010) describes the process of moving from known to unknown when working with culturally and linguistically diverse students. She urges teachers to listen in a variety of ways to what students share about their background experiences so that the activities we present to them are comprehensible. It is only in this way that instruction becomes meaningful. Examples of how we listen to what students bring to class include reading their writing, discussing their illustrations, asking them about their experiences, and providing many opportunities for them to interpret in their own words the content being studied in the classroom.

Here are four simple activities that may be used over and over in the classroom to connect students' writing to the language and vocabulary they know and their out-of-school experiences. At the same time these learning experiences give teachers a richer portrait of each student's complexity and strength.

TELL A STORY TO GET A STORY (McCabe & Bliss, 2003). When you are meeting with a small or large group of students, recount a dramatic event you experienced. Examples might be a time you got hurt, lost something, or had a fun time. Don't be afraid to use emotion and descriptive language. When you have finished telling the story, ask students to tell a story like that to a partner and then have them write or draw about what they shared. Emergent and alphabetic writers can dictate their stories to an adult after they have illustrated it.

LANGUAGE EXPERIENCE APPROACH (Stauffer, 1980). As a class or in a small group, provide a hands-on or "being there" experience that is memorable and encourages students to use language. Examples include cooking, observing wildlife or weather, or working collaboratively on a construction project. Use words that express how the activity looks, sounds, smells, feels, or tastes. After completing the experience, have students write about or illustrate what happened. Frame sentences can guide the writing for students who need extra support.

RESPOND TO CULTURALLY RELEVANT LITERATURE (DeNicolo & Franquiz, 2006). Find children's literature that reflects the backgrounds and life experiences of some of your students. Have students discuss this material in small book groups and then write about their reactions in a journal. Over time students will gain a greater understanding of diverse perspectives as they put themselves in the place of the narrator and have opportunities to hear their classmates' responses.

INVITE FAMILY MEMBERS INTO WRITING WORKSHOP (Allen, 2010). After choosing a writing form such as a poem, photo essay, or story, model how the writing proceeds. Invite family members in to either do the writing with students or send materials home and have students bring them back to school. Provide clear directions in English and students' home languages. This is an excellent way to bring the voices of family members into the classroom community.

As you review students' writing, you may notice that their home language surfaces in their English writing. For instance, some students experience difficulties distinguishing and representing sounds that do not exist in their home language (e.g., confusions between /ch/ and /sh/ for Spanish speakers or /l/ and /r/ for speakers of some Asian languages). When you notice similar errors in the work of students from the same language backgrounds, take the time to meet with them as a small group to clarify the confusions (Helman, 2005). Let students share with you the parts of English that are difficult for them and how these features are different from their home languages.

Another area that may come up in students' writing is a tendency to use a story structure that is different from the Western classroom focus on direct, concise story lines. Many cultures use story narratives that are

FIGURE 5.6. Writing and Word Study Activities

Activity	Explanation "I do"	Guidance "We do"	Practice "You do"
Sentence frame (Dutro & Helman, 2009)	Teacher creates the stem of a sentence for the students to complete. Teacher models how sentences are put together.	Students assist the teacher or a partner to create novel sentences. Teacher provides feedback and assistance.	Students construct their own sentences and write them into their writer's notebooks.
Personal readers	Teacher helps students memorize a poem or short piece of text by reading it many times.	A copy of the text is placed in a folder for students to reread to the teacher or other mentor.	Students come back to the memorized text over and over to find interesting words, identify frame sentences, or cut apart sentences to put in order.
Picture or word sorting (Helman et al., 2012)	Teacher models a sound, pattern, or meaning sort at students' developmental level.	Students join in to sort items as the teacher guides the process.	Students do the sort on their own or with a buddy. When fluent, they write or glue their sort in a word study notebook.
Demonstrating and conferring about writing (Calkins, 2011)	Teacher identifies an area for growth in students' writing and models a related mini-lesson.	Together teacher and students review past writing efforts to apply the new learning. Teacher confers with students who need support as they write.	Students write and take into account learning from the mini-lesson. After the writing workshop, students share their work with a partner.
Content dictations	Teacher reads a piece of informational text related to content being studied in class. Students listen and take in all the information they can.	Students discuss what they remember with a partner or in a teacher-led small group. Students then write the content in their own words (less proficient writers dictate the information to a mentor).	Students reread the dictation and create illustrations. They can use this writing in future informational text writing.

more character-centered and have a circular storytelling line (McCabe & Bliss, 2003). These narratives may seem repetitive to teachers who feel that students are "not getting anywhere." As educators work to help all students meet rigorous standards for advanced use of written language in explanatory and creative texts, it will help to understand the narratives

FIGURE 5.7. Authentic Writing Activities

Write a letter to a parent	Write a book review	Write a joke	Write directions
Make a shopping list	Keep a journal	Create a survey	Write a song
Write a scary story	Write a poem	Write a favorite TV personality	Write a recipe
Create an interactive home–school journal	Design a bumper sticker	Write a letter to the teacher	Write a play
Write a report about your favorite animal	Write an advertisement	Write a video game	Write to a politician
Write to the school principal	Write a letter to a friend	Write an autobiography	Create a crossword puzzle
Write captions for a photo album	Write to complain about a problem	Write to thank someone for their help	Write your goals

students have internalized from their home cultures. That way, we can be respectful and appreciative of the different styles that are part of students' ways of being, create hybrid events that combine what students bring with school goals, and build a bridge for students to meet academic expectations (Au, 2009).

Use Modeling and Explicit Instruction

Students who are learning oral English, or who have limited exposure to the structures of academic language presented in texts, benefit from seeing multiple examples and having opportunities to discuss the patterns or regularities in oral or written language. For example, if students are asked to create an informational text with facts, definitions, and details, they will profit from seeing and analyzing some examples of statements and from getting feedback as they make initial writing attempts. Explicit instruction involves a cycle of explanation and practice that incorporates writing skills and the language encompassed by the writing task (Snow & Katz, 2010). Another way to frame the idea of modeling and explicit instruction is to describe the release of responsibility in teaching from "I do" to "we do" to "you do" (Dutro & Helman, 2009). Figure 5.6 outlines a number of writing and word study activities that fit well into an explicit instruction model and scaffold students to higher standards.

Provide Opportunities to Write for Authentic Purposes

Aside from getting a grade, many students who are reluctant writers don't see the point of school-based writing. To increase motivation and demonstrate the importance of writing in "real life," plan writing activities that are authentic and meaningful for your students. After doing many of the activities outlined in this chapter, you likely will have a much better idea of how to connect writing to the values and experiences of your students. Figure 5.7 reveals a quilt of possible ideas for authentic writing in your classroom.

SUMMARY

Beyond the learning that students derive from writing, their products also provide an amazing source of authentic assessment for teachers. Teachers can save examples of student writing throughout the school year to document their students' learning. The artifacts of writing tell us about our students' capabilities with oral and written language, and give us clues about what to focus instruction on next. When students write artifacts, they teach their teachers about their interests, backgrounds, and dreams. Writing captures so much of who we are as people, and who we want to become. Let writing help you understand your students and engage them in literacy.

CHAPTER 6

Informal Assessments That Guide Literacy Instruction

IN CURRENT POLICY debates about schooling, assessment seems to have become a lightning rod among educators, politicians, parents, and other stakeholders. Some feel that we are testing children too much or that we aren't testing the right proficiencies; others believe that summative evaluations of student learning are the key to ensuring that all students meet the benchmarks that predict future success (Afflerbach, 2011). The one thing most everyone can agree on is that the accountability systems that are in place for schools, teachers, and students will not be going away soon. Still, while adults discuss and question the role of large-scale testing in schools, no one is disputing that ongoing, formative assessment is essential to good teaching. Formative assessment provides valuable information about students' strengths and pinpoints areas for growth. If teachers don't know what a student is able to do, how will we know how to challenge that student at an appropriate level?

FOUR PURPOSES OF ASSESSMENT

At Carrie's school in a large urban district, she finds that she has more data on her students' reading proficiencies than ever before. Students are "screened" at the beginning of the year with a 1-minute fluency assessment; they are given standardized tests of reading comprehension and vocabulary twice a year; and they also must take a set of grade-level assessments three times a year. At the end of the first few weeks of school, Carrie knows who is not meeting grade-level benchmarks, but does not know exactly what to do next. Before discussing how teachers like Carrie can best use informal assessments to guide their literacy instruction, it is important to be clear about different purposes for assessments. Assessments can be used to evaluate school programs and curriculum, to screen students who may need extra support, to monitor students' progress, and to inform instructional decision making.

Assessment for Program Evaluation

One purpose of assessment is to document how educational systems are working for students overall at the classroom, school, district, and state levels. Large-scale, standardized tests that are required by state or federal institutions are designed to show strengths or weaknesses at a macro level. They are often used to reward or punish educational systems that are meeting or failing to meet policymakers' standards for growth through legislation such as No Child Left Behind. However, large-scale standardized assessments such as the National Assessment of Educational Progress help bring to light important information about achievement gaps across various populations in our educational systems (U.S. Department of Education, 2010). For example, in 2010, 86% of White third graders in Minnesota scored at a proficient level on the statewide reading exam, compared with 58% of Black students and 55% of Hispanic students. That is a proficiency gap of 28% and 21%, respectively, between White and Black students and White and Hispanic students. This gap persists through each grade level, and by tenth grade the difference between the proficiency rates of Black and White students is 35% (Minnesota Department of Education, 2011). Without program evaluation assessments, the need to address this gap would not be apparent. Data from program evaluation assessments are not designed to provide instructional information at the individual student level.

Assessment for Screening

Another important role for assessment is to quickly identify, or screen, students who are not meeting grade-level expectations early on so that they can receive additional support. Typical screening measures vary by grade level. For instance, a kindergarten screening measure might evaluate alphabet knowledge or the ability to identify beginning sounds in words spoken aloud. A first-grade screening tool is likely to involve letter–sound correspondences or high-frequency word recognition. And second- to sixth-grade screening tools frequently involve students reading a graded passage for 1 minute to check their reading rate. While screening assessments may give teachers some indication of a student's literacy capabilities, that is not their primary purpose. They are designed to sort students who are "doing okay" from those who "need more help" to meet grade-level performance expectations.

Screening tools do not provide much diagnostic information. If a third-grade student reads the screening passage at a rate below the cutoff score, the only thing the teacher knows is that something is not working for the student. So, screening serves as an important first step, but must always be followed by a deeper look into why the student is underperforming, and what may be done to help the student progress more rapidly.

Assessment for Monitoring Students' Progress

It is not enough to screen students once a year to identify those who are struggling. Ongoing assessment is necessary to ensure that students maintain a successful learning trajectory and that students who have been identified as needing help are responding to the tailored instruction they receive. Progress-monitoring assessments vary by grade level and might include measures of alphabetic skills; ratings of fluency, accuracy, and comprehension on short pieces of text; and developmental spelling checks. Progress monitoring should occur frequently, and it should assess the particular literacy area of concern for the student. For example, a second-grade student who has not yet developed fluent and automatic decoding skills will need to be assessed frequently, using short, timed reading passages and including a brief comprehension check. A kindergarten student who is developing letter recognition will need to be assessed frequently on knowledge of the alphabet. Students of all grade levels with limited vocabulary and oral language skills need to be monitored for their comprehension of texts in written or oral form.

A key partner to progress monitoring is using the data collected to provide the right level of support for students who are not making good growth on grade-level benchmarks. Ongoing monitoring of students' progress guides teachers in understanding that "one size does not fit all" in literacy teaching and learning. If a student is not successful, we need to identify additional or different types of instruction that may have a greater impact, and then we must continue to monitor progress to verify that this instruction is working. Students who are not thriving when instruction is delivered in larger group settings will need tailored instruction in small groups. Students who still do not progress toward grade-level benchmarks within leveled, small-group instruction may need focused instruction on a more individualized level.

Assessment for Instructional Decision Making

A crucial purpose of literacy assessment is to help teachers plan instruction that starts from what students can do and ends with students accomplishing their grade-level performance expectations. Assessments to guide instruction may take a variety of forms, including listening to students read the text being studied, examining their independent work following a lesson, checking for understanding within a teacher-guided lesson, or embedding brief quizzes relating to the content being learned. For example, a teacher may look for speed and accuracy as students sort their words in word study, ask comprehension questions as a student reads a text, or review students' summaries of key ideas in a book club or thematic text. Teachers often ask students to give an example of what they were studying as an "exit ticket" before they transition to a new activity. Young students can provide an oral example as a quick check of their knowledge of a skill or concept. For example, a kindergarten or first-grade student might be asked, "Point to a word that starts like the sound you hear at the beginning of *dog*." These informal assessments measure student understanding and proficiency in grade-level skills and tell teachers whether and when students are ready to move on to more challenging work. They also signal whether students need more guidance and instruction to have success with the learning objectives.

While many assessments for instructional decision making may seem more like instruction than assessment, it is important that teachers are intentional about using them. Some students, especially English language learners, are very good at "hiding out" in class—sometimes even when we work with them in small groups. Regular, documented observations of students' learning through running records of reading, spell checks, quick writes, or vocabulary questions are essential to making sure that students are keeping up with the curriculum and ready to move forward. These checks of student learning should be conducted as often as possible, and at least once per week. After a month of instruction, it is too late to find out that students are not grasping the skills and content under study.

THE TEACHER'S ROLE IN LITERACY ASSESSMENT

Your role in collecting, scoring, and analyzing assessment data will vary depending on the resources and requirements of your school district. In Carrie's district, teachers have some support when conducting the initial screening of students to see whether they are meeting grade-level reading benchmarks. This means that the reading specialist joins her to conduct 1-minute oral reading proficiency checks with all of her students. Three times a year, Carrie is also responsible for gathering data on students' developmental spelling and their proficiency on a set of leveled reading passages. Kindergarten and first-grade teachers in her district give letter recognition, phonics, and phonemic awareness assessments, as well.

Once the assessments have been conducted, Carrie meets with her grade-level colleagues to go over the results. The school is working on a plan to provide additional support to students who are screened as "below benchmark." In addition, Carrie and her colleagues discuss teaching approaches or collaboration practices that may help them address the developmental levels of each of their academically diverse students. All members of the school team are committed to ensuring that they base their instruction on multiple measures of student progress and that each student's literacy abilities grow as quickly as possible. Between district-required assessment dates, Carrie and her colleagues rely on informal assessments of student learning to guide their teaching practice.

WHAT IS AN INFORMAL ASSESSMENT?

Informal assessments are selected or created by teachers and school personnel to gather information about students' learning in classroom settings (Lipson & Wixson, 2009). In contrast to norm-referenced or standardized tests, informal assessments are connected to specific learning outcomes in particular classrooms and schools. Informal assessments often are embedded in classroom instruction and help teachers gain insight into the extent to which students know and are applying literacy skills and strategies. Because informal assessments are frequent and mimic classroom instruction, they represent a more authentic picture of student learning.

INFORMAL ASSESSMENTS AT EACH DEVELOPMENTAL LEVEL

Just as one lesson plan or one instructional text does not fit every student, the same may be said about literacy assessments. An important goal of formal and informal assessments is to pinpoint where students are in terms of their literacy development and to reveal what steps are needed to carry students forward. For example, students at the emergent level of literacy development are learning to recognize and name the letters of the alphabet and are gaining an understanding of how words in spoken language can be broken into separate sounds (phonemic awareness). Emergent readers memorize some basic high-frequency words, gain familiarity with features of print, and begin to match their spoken words to printed words on the page in memorized texts (Morris, Bloodgood, Lomax, & Perney, 2003). By assessing these important milestones in literacy development, teachers learn what instructional activities are important to propel students forward.

In this chapter I present assessment "menus" that connect to students' developmental levels in reading and writing, as outlined in Chapters 4 and 5. Each menu presents the most critical classroom-based informal assessments of students' reading, writing, listening, and speaking skills at that particular level of literacy development. Remember, developmental level does not mean grade level. A fourth-grade classroom may have students who represent several literacy developmental levels from beginning to advanced readers. So, once you have determined through screening assessments that students are not able to be successful in the grade-level materials, developmentally appropriate assessments should be used to identify exactly what competencies each student has and what type of instruction will be most beneficial for that student. For this reason, a fourth-grade teacher may need to use informal assessments from a variety of developmental levels.

On the following pages an informal assessment menu is laid out for students at the emergent, beginning, transitional, intermediate, and advanced reading levels. These menus name and describe several key language and literacy informal assessments, outline procedures for their implementation, describe student behaviors to look for, and suggest next steps in instruction based on student performance. These assessment menus are not designed to be all-encompassing. Rather, they provide an introduction to several research-based, high-impact informal assessments that fit naturally into classroom practices and provide important information to tailor literacy instruction for every student.

Informal Assessments for Emergent Learners

Emergent readers are learning oral vocabulary and language structures rapidly and are beginning to make connections between spoken and written language. Knowledge of the letters of the alphabet is key to learners at this stage because it provides initial information about letter–sound correspondences that can be used to begin to recognize or write printed words. At first, emergent learners are "pretending" to read memorized texts and are mimicking writing by stringing together letters or letter-like figures. A key goal of informal assessments at the emergent level is to identify the transition from pre-alphabetic to early alphabetic reading and writing skills. In other words, we want to know when students stop memorizing words as pictures and begin to use their knowledge of letters and sounds as tools in reading and writing tasks. Figure 6.1, which is located in the Appendix at the end of the chapter, outlines several of the most critical informal assessments for emergent readers and writers. Descriptions of how to conduct the assessments, expected student performance, and suggestions for further instruction are included.

Informal Assessments for Beginning Readers

Beginning readers are able to read simple texts using a combination of sight-word reading and phonics skills. Beginning readers have not yet developed fluency. They tend to read word by word in a somewhat labored manner, especially as they are using their growing phonics skills for decoding. The period of beginning reading might best be described as a training period: Students strengthen their phonemic awareness and phonics muscles as they read many, many words and simple texts. By the end of the beginning reading stage, students have developed a more fluent pace and automatically decode words that contain more complex phonics patterns. To assess beginning readers, teachers use measures of phonics and phonemic awareness, and look for a full concept of word, alphabetic spelling behaviors, and attempts to use more varied text structures in student writing. Because beginning reading materials tend to be simplified for student readability, they generally are not good materials to measure higher level thinking about texts. For this reason it is still important to orally assess comprehension of stories or informational books. Figure 6.2 outlines some of the most important informal assessments for beginning readers and writers.

Informal Assessments for Transitional Readers

Transitional readers have become much more automatic in their decoding and now have greater access to texts of a variety of genres. Transitional students generally read between 70 and 100 words per minute in grade-level materials and write two paragraphs of text with greater fluency (although still with plenty of spelling errors). Transitional students have mastered sound–symbol relationships in the writing system, but they are working to understand and use the vowel spelling patterns of more complex phonics patterns. By the end of the transitional stage, students are reading extended chapter books, newspapers, and web-based content, and they have formed preferences for genres of reading materials based on topics of personal interest. To assess transitional readers, teachers use measures of oral reading fluency, accuracy, and comprehension. Because of students' expanded decoding skills, vocabulary and comprehension of content can be assessed through written texts as well. Developmental spelling inventories assess students' growing knowledge of the spelling, phonics, and meaning of words. With expanding writing skills, students can now create pieces of writing that demonstrate their capabilities in a number of areas, including conveying ideas and information, using creativity, establishing a structure for their text, and participating in a writing process to strengthen their work (Council of Chief State School Officers, 2010). Figure 6.3 outlines some of the most important informal assessments for transitional readers and writers.

Informal Assessments for Intermediate Readers

Intermediate readers are reading silently and automatically in a variety of genres. These students generally read more than 100 words per minute in young adult materials and write extended pieces of text with fluency (although still with some errors in spelling multisyllabic words). Intermediate students have mastered most spelling patterns in single-syllable words and are developing an understanding of how syllables are joined in words and how words are changed by affixes. By the end of the intermediate stage of reading, students are reading adult-level materials and have developed preferences and habits in their reading behaviors. To assess intermediate readers, teachers evaluate their comprehension of the reading material. This can be done through discussion or in writing. Developmental spelling inventories assess students' growing knowledge of the spelling and meanings of words. With advancing writing skills, students can now create pieces of writing that demonstrate their capabilities in a number of areas, including conveying ideas and information clearly and coherently, using evidence, choosing descriptive language and domain-specific vocabulary, using dialogue, and establishing a structure for their text (including a conclusion), and they strengthen their work by planning, revising, and editing (Council of Chief State School Officers, 2010). Figure 6.4 (see Appendix at end of chapter) outlines some of the most important informal assessments for intermediate readers and writers.

WHAT TO DO IF YOU DON'T KNOW A STUDENT'S DEVELOPMENTAL LEVEL

There is not a one-to-one correspondence between grade level and development, so you may find that you need a quick way to pinpoint a student's development before beginning informal assessment. One efficient way to assess students' developmental levels is to give a brief spelling inventory, as described in Chapter 5 (Bear et al., 2012). After using this assessment you will have a good idea of whether students are operating at the emergent, beginning, transitional, or intermediate level of literacy development. Based on the results of the spelling inventory, use the appropriate literacy assessments, as outlined in Figures 6.1–6.3 in the appendix at the end of the chapter. This will help you to get right to the heart of students' instructional needs in reading, writing, and language development.

SUMMARY

Informal assessments are an important source of information to guide in-structional planning. The assessments outlined in this chapter give teachers information about students' oral language and breadth of vocabulary; their knowledge of phonics, the alphabet, and words; and their reading and writing development. Students will learn best when academic material is within their instructional level. After conducting informal assessments, teachers should cluster students into groups based on common proficiencies and needs. As students progress, the learning groups should be reconstituted so that each student is appropriately challenged. Because the assessments in this chapter are based on typical classroom activities, each assessment suggests the types of learning activities that are most fitting.

APPENDIX

Figures 6.1–6.4 are on the following pages.

FIGURE 6.1. Informal Assessments for Emergent Readers and Writers

Assessment	How It Is Done	What to Look for in Students	If Students Need Additional Help in This Area
Oral language	Talk with students one-on-one to hear their communication skills in English. Or, conduct focused observations of students as they take turns communicating in partnerships with their peers. Enlist the help of bilingual personnel or volunteers to speak with English learners and gauge their proficiency in the home language.	Listen for students' ability to communicate ideas. Do they struggle for words or sentence structures to express their thoughts? What can your bilingual resource person elucidate about students' home language proficiency and usage?	Provide a separate time in the day to work with students who need explicit language development in English. Use the home language of English learners to help students understand instruction and contribute to classroom activities. Structure partner and small-group activities throughout the day so that students have many opportunities to practice using oral language in meaningful ways.
Vocabulary	Frequently check to see whether students know the meanings of important words used in the classroom. Ask them to use these words in a sentence or to say what they know about the words. In shared reading, ask students to find and point to key items they are reading about.	Note the important words that students cannot point to, use in a sentence, or describe. Is limited vocabulary knowledge causing students to substitute pronouns such as *that, this one*, and so on, to express themselves? Notice the behaviors students use when they do not know the meaning of a word. Do they ask for help from a friend or teacher, or simply ignore the word?	Explicitly introduce three to five of the most important words in each shared reading or mini-lesson and use them repeatedly throughout. Provide many visuals to help students learn the meaning of words in their studies. Let students know that they should ask for help from friends or teachers when they do not understand what a word means.
Chanting or singing the alphabet	Ask students whether they can sing or tell you the alphabet.	Note the accuracy of order and pronunciation of letter names. Can students get all the way to the end?	Provide guided practice every day. Have child-sized alphabet charts for students to read along with. Use recorded songs or chants for students to listen to on their own.
Letter recognition	Use either a printed page or a set of uppercase (or lowercase) letters in mixed-up order. Point to each letter and ask students to say its name.	Note the letters that students can name and those they can't. Write down any letter recognition confusions students have.	Use the names of fellow students or important words to practice identifying letter names in context. Engage with many alphabet manipulatives during word study. Provide tools such as alphabet cards and ABC books for students to reference throughout the day.

FIGURE 6.1. Informal Assessments for Emergent Readers and Writers, Continued

Assessment	How It Is Done	What to Look for in Students	If Students Need Additional Help in This Area
Phonological awareness	Use picture cards to have students identify words that rhyme with or begin like a key picture. Or, have students sort pictures into two or three columns based on their beginning sounds (Helman, Bear, Invernizzi, Templeton, & Johnston, 2009a).	Listen as students say the words aloud and match them to a key picture. Are they able to pull the onset or rime off of the whole word? Note: This is also a great assessment of vocabulary knowledge.	Plan a systematic series of word study lessons that begins with sorting easier pictures such as those with continuous sounds ($/f/, /l/, /m/, /n/, /r/, /s/,$ or $/v/$) or sorting pictures that have clear contrasts (such as $/m/$ and $/s/$). Keep track of students' growth so that you can continuously build on what they know as you add more challenges.
Concepts about print (Clay, 2006)	Ask students to point out features of text as they handle a simple picture book, such as the front of the book, the title and author, an illustration, a word, a letter, a period, and so on. Have students show you what part of the page they read, the direction in which text is read, and what they do when they get to the end of a page.	Look for confidence in book handling: Is the book right side up, can students page through from front to back, and so on? Note students' familiarity with identifying letters, words, and punctuation marks.	Students who have limited experiences handling books and listening to read-aloud stories may need more explicit support in understanding the features of print. Model concepts about print in small-group writing lessons and shared big book reading. Provide opportunities for guided practice in identifying features of print in small, leveled reading lessons.
Developmental spelling	Ask students to spell a few simple words (e.g., single-syllable words without digraphs or blends) "the best they can" (Helman, et al., 2009a).	Are students using scribbles, letter-like figures, or real letters? Do their samples include any use of spelling–sound correspondences?	Students who are using scribble writing or letter-like figures should receive numerous opportunities to examine print through shared reading and writing and alphabetic activities. Students who are using real letters and beginning to make spelling–sound correspondences should be encouraged to use their writing skills as much as possible and should begin to receive systematic early phonics instruction.
Writing	After modeling an example, ask students to write a story in whatever form they are able to.	Note directionality, spacing, and other concepts about print. Are students representing words with shapes, letters, or words? What literate language or background knowledge is evident in their messages?	Students need the freedom to make mistakes and write "their way." The more they write, the more you will understand their development. Build on whatever alphabetic, storytelling, or fine motor skills your students are demonstrating to take them another step forward. (Calkins, 2005)

Assessment	How It Is Done	What to Look for in Students	If Students Need Additional Help in This Area
Letter-sound knowledge	Use either a printed page or a set of uppercase (or lowercase) letters in mixed-up order. Point to each letter and ask students to say what sound it makes.	Note the letter sounds that students can name and those they can't. Write down any sound–symbol confusions students have.	Build on the letter–sound correspondences that your students know to systematically introduce and compare new letters and their sounds. Begin with clear contrasts, especially for students from language backgrounds other than English. Use visuals to simultaneously build vocabulary and phonics knowledge.
Concept of word (COW)	After students have learned a simple rhyme by heart, have them read and point to the text of the rhyme to see whether they can match what they are saying to the words in print. To be effective, some of the words in this task need to be multisyllabic (Bear et al., 2012).	Look for some orientation to the page for students who are just developing COW. They may move left to right and top to bottom in general motions, but their reading may not match their pointing. As students develop rudimentary COW, their finger pointing becomes more precise, but they may still get off track, especially with multisyllabic words.	Provide lots of chart stories, big books, or other large-type printed materials for students to read along to. Take the time to help students orally learn the rhyme or dictation and then engage in repeated, supported readings. Encourage students to look at the text as they read and try to match what they know about a word to its form in print.
Oral comprehension	While reading aloud to students, stop periodically to ask the group to make predictions about what will happen next or to make textual connections. This is best done in small groups so all students' voices are included, but partner sharing also permits everyone to express their ideas.	If students are sharing with a partner, listen in on one or two groups and note whether students are showing that they have understood the material and can draw on their own background knowledge to make connections. Are students making thoughtful predictions, or do they seem disconnected from the content of the material?	Students who have difficulty making meaning of the read-aloud texts in class may need to work in smaller groups with material that is closer to their listening comprehension level. Try to find out what is impeding student understanding: Is it unfamiliar vocabulary and/or complex language structures that make understanding difficult? Is a limited background experience in the topic or lack of interest a factor? Would a more relevant or visually engaging text support students' access to the material?

FIGURE 6.2. Informal Assessments for Beginning Readers and Writers

Assessment	How It Is Done	What to Look for in Students	If Students Need Additional Help in This Area
Oral language	Talk with students one-on-one to hear their communication skills in English. Or, conduct focused observations of students as they take turns communicating in partnerships with their peers. Enlist the help of bilingual personnel or volunteers to speak with English learners and gauge their proficiency in the home language.	Listen for students' ability to communicate ideas. Do they struggle for words or sentence structures to express their thoughts? What can your bilingual resource person elucidate about students' home language development?	Provide a separate time in the day to work with students who need explicit language development in English. Use the home language of English learners to help students understand instruction and contribute to classroom activities. Structure partner and small-group activities throughout the day so that students have many opportunities to practice using oral language in meaningful ways.
Vocabulary	Frequently check to see whether students know the meanings of important words used in the classroom. Ask them to use these words in a sentence or to say what they know about each word. In shared and guided reading, ask students to find and point to key items they are reading about.	Note the important words that students cannot point to, use in a sentence, or describe. Is limited vocabulary knowledge causing students to substitute pronouns such as *that, this one,* and so on, to express themselves? Notice the behaviors students use when they do not know the meaning of a word. Do they ask for help from a friend or teacher, or simply ignore the word?	Explicitly introduce three to five of the most important words in each reading or writing lesson. Provide many visuals to help students learn the meanings of words in their studies. Let students know that they should ask for help from friends or teachers when they do not understand what a word means.
Literacy skills in a home language	Confer with individual students about their background literacy experiences in a home language. Ask students to read or write a story in their home language. Encourage them to "show you what they know" in a home language if they have not had formal instruction.	Look for fluency in reading and writing in students' home language. Ask students how they think knowing how to read and write in their home language will help them learn English. Find a bilingual resource person who can help you assess students' literacy in their home language.	Students who bring background literacy skills from their home language will be able to make lots of connections to reading and writing in English. Research the similarities across the two languages or get input from a bilingual resource person. Help students to connect what they know in a home language to reading and writing in English.
Developmental spelling	Ask students to spell "the best they can" a set of words that contain progressively more difficult features. For example, start with spelling simple short vowel words and progress to words with complex vowel patterns (see Bear et al., 2012).	Note the features that students use correctly such as beginning or ending sounds, short vowel sounds, or blends and digraphs. When students make attempts that are not always correct, that informs you as to where to begin phonics and spelling instruction.	Students' spelling samples tell you where you need to begin instruction. Find the picture or word sorts that practice the phonic elements that students are "using but confusing."

Assessment	How It Is Done	What to Look for in Students	If Students Need Additional Help in This Area
Writing	After reading a variety of texts in a particular genre, and modeling this same type of writing for students, invite them to write their own piece. Genres may include narrative, informational, or poetic styles.	Depending on the genre under study, look for students' idea development, language use, word choice, and voice (see Pinnell & Fountas, 2007). As students become more advanced beginning readers, assess their use of print conventions such as punctuation, spacing, and capitalization.	Students who have difficulty adhering to the features of a particular genre may need more explicit outlines or frame sentences to structure their writing. Mini-lessons can help reinforce students' use of conventions in their writing. Language experience activities are good ways to provide content for writing in a variety of genres.
Letter–sound knowledge	Use a printed page of uppercase (or lowercase) letters in mixed-up order. Point to each letter and ask students to say what sound it makes.	Note the letter sounds that students can name and those they can't. Write down any sound–symbol confusions students have.	Build on the letter–sound correspondences that your students know to systematically introduce and compare new letters and their sounds. Begin with clear contrasts, especially for students from language backgrounds other than English (see Helman, Bear, Invernizzi, Templeton, & Johnston, 2009b). Use visuals to simultaneously build vocabulary and phonics knowledge.
Concept of word (COW)	Use memorized rhymes, dictations, or other simple texts to see whether students can match what they are saying to the words in print. To be effective, some of the words in this task need to be multisyllabic (see Bear et al., 2012).	Look for students to have a full COW at this stage. Their finger pointing matches the text accurately, and if they get off track, they can correct themselves without having to start the passage over.	Encourage students to reread pieces of text many times and to look at the text as they read while matching what they know about a word to its form in print. Encourage students to remember high-frequency words by sight, instead of trying to sound them out each time.
Sight word knowledge	Prepare a list of the first 100 high-frequency words (or use a list your district supplies). Ask students to read as many of these words as they can automatically by sight. Skip to a new word if the student cannot read a word quickly.	Look for beginning readers to steadily grow in the number of high-frequency words they recognize—early beginning readers should recognize about 10 words and late beginning readers will read between 100 and 200.	Students who are not becoming automatic in their reading of high-frequency words need more opportunities to read simple texts that contain these words. They also can use these words in games, sorts, word walls, and sentence-building activities.
Running record of reading behaviors (Clay, 2010)	Observe students one-on-one as they read a passage of text aloud. Note reading behaviors such as any miscues (omissions or substitutions of words), self-corrections, and pacing. Also keep a record of the types of strategies students use when they get to an unknown word.	Look for cues to better understanding each student's reading performance and strategies. Is the student using phonics to decode or relying on sight words and context clues? Is the chosen text at the student's independent, instructional, or frustration level?	Running records show teachers whether students are having success in a given text. If a text is overwhelming to a student, help select an easier level or another text in which the student has more background knowledge. Periodically use running records with students to ensure they are reading "just right" materials.

FIGURE 6.2. Informal Assessments for Beginning Readers and Writers, Continued

Assessment	How It Is Done	What to Look for in Students	If Students Need Additional Help in This Area
Oral reading fluency	Select a passage of about 120 words from grade-level reading materials or a school or district standardized measure. Ask students to read the passage for 1 minute. Subtract any words that were not read correctly to calculate students' words correct per minute score.	This assessment is a quick way to screen students to see whether they are meeting school benchmarks for reading fluency. By the end of the beginning reading stage, students should be reading approximately 60 to 70 words correct per minute.	If students are not meeting the oral reading fluency benchmark set by your school, it is important to dig deeper to see what is holding the students back. A beginning reader who is having trouble developing fluency will likely need additional work in phonics to make word reading more automatic.
Oral comprehension	Read aloud a grade-level passage and then ask students to answer specific comprehension questions or have them retell the main events from the text.	Look for accurate or reasonable answers to your comprehension questions. Students who retell the passage should be able to share major events in an appropriate sequence. Students should be able to answer inferential as well as literal questions.	Students who have difficulty with oral comprehension may need extra support in the area of language or vocabulary development. They also could be confused by information that differs or is absent from their personal background experiences. Provide extra scaffolding in any of these areas as needed.

FIGURE 6.3. Informal Assessments for Transitional Readers and Writers

Assessment	How It Is Done	What to Look for in Students	If Students Need Additional Help in This Area
Oral language	Talk with students one-on-one to hear their use of vocabulary and academic language in English. Or, conduct focused observations of students as they communicate in partnerships during academic activities. Enlist the help of bilingual personnel or volunteers to speak with English learners and gauge their proficiency in the home language.	Listen for students' ability to communicate ideas. Do they struggle for words or sentence structures to express their understanding of learning objectives? What can your bilingual resource person elucidate about students' home language development?	Provide a separate time in the day to work with students who need explicit language development in English. Use the home language of English learners to help students understand instruction and contribute to classroom activities. Structure partner and small-group activities throughout the day so that students have many opportunities to practice using oral language in meaningful ways.
Vocabulary	Frequently check to see whether students know the meanings of important words used in the classroom. Ask them to use these words in a sentence or to say what they know about each word. In guided and independent reading, ask students to describe key topics they are reading about.	Note the important words that students cannot use in a sentence or describe. Is limited vocabulary knowledge causing students to substitute pronouns such as *that, this one*, and so on, to express themselves? Notice the behaviors students use when they do not know the meaning of a word. Do they ask for help from a friend or teacher, or simply ignore the word?	Work explicitly with five to seven of the most important words in each literacy lesson. Provide many visuals to help students learn the meanings of words in their content studies. Develop graphic organizers to help students perceive the slight variations in a continuum of related words (e.g., *angry, furious, enraged*). Let students know that they should seek help when they do not understand what a word means.

FIGURE 6.3. Informal Assessments for Transitional Readers and Writers. Continued

Assessment	How It Is Done	What to Look for in Students	If Students Need Additional Help in This Area
Literacy skills in a home language	Conference with individual students about their background literacy experiences in a home language. Ask students to read or write a story in their home language. Encourage them to share what they know in their home language.	Look for fluency in reading and writing in students' home language. Ask students how they think knowing how to read and write in their home language will help them learn English. Find a bilingual resource person who can help you assess students' literacy in their home language.	Students who bring background literacy skills from their home language will be able to make lots of connections to reading and writing in English. Research the similarities across the two languages or get input from a bilingual resource person. Help students to connect what they know in a home language to reading and writing in English.
Developmental spelling	Ask students to spell "the best they can" a set of words that contain progressively more difficult features, for example, moving from spelling short vowel words to spelling words with complex vowel patterns or inflected endings (see Bear et al., 2012).	Note the features that students use correctly, such as long vowel patterns, other vowels, or inflected endings. When students make attempts that are not always correct, that informs you as to where to begin word study instruction.	Students' spelling samples tell you where you need to begin instruction. Introduce the word sorts that practice the spelling patterns that students are "using but confusing."
Writing	After reading a variety of texts in a particular genre, and modeling this same type of writing for students, invite them to write their own piece. Genres may include narrative, informational, or poetic styles.	Depending on the genre under study, look for students' idea development, language structure, word choice, and description (see Pinnell & Fountas, 2007). As students develop more writing fluency, listen for voice, clarity, or imagination in their writing.	Students who have difficulty adhering to the features of a particular genre may need more explicit outlines or frame sentences to structure their writing. Graphic organizers can help students make a plan for their writing. They also provide a reference for ideas throughout the writing process.

Assessment	How It Is Done	What to Look for in Students	If Students Need Additional Help in This Area
Oral reading fluency	Select a passage of about 120 words from grade-level reading materials or a school or district standardized measure. Ask students to read the passage for 1 minute. Subtract any words that were not read correctly from students' words correct per minute score.	This assessment is a quick way to screen students to see whether they are meeting school benchmarks for reading fluency. Early transitional readers should read about 70 words per minute. As students advance in this stage, they come to prefer silent reading and read at rates closer to 100 words per minute.	If students are not meeting the oral reading fluency benchmark set by your school, it is important to dig deeper to see what is holding the students back. Some students may stumble on words, others may not yet have developed automaticity, and still others may be lacking comprehension (see Valencia & Buly, 2004).
Running record of reading behaviors (see Clay, 2010)	Observe students one-on-one as they read a passage of text aloud. Note reading behaviors such as any miscues (omissions or substitutions of words), self-corrections, and pacing. Also keep a record of the types of strategies students use when they get to an unknown word.	Look for cues to better understanding each student's reading performance and strategies. Is the student using phonics to decode or relying on sight words and context clues? Is the chosen text at the student's independent, instructional, or frustration level?	Running records show teachers whether students are having success in a given text. If a text is overwhelming to a student, help select an easier level or another text in which the student has more background knowledge. Periodically use running records with students to ensure they are reading "just right" materials.
Reading comprehension	After students have read a section of text, ask them to answer specific comprehension questions or make a prediction about what may happen next. Students also can retell or write a summary of their reading.	Look for accurate or reasonable answers to your comprehension questions in students' predictions. Students also should be able to answer inferential questions. Students who retell or summarize the passage should be able to share major events in an appropriate sequence.	Students who have difficulty with reading comprehension may need extra support in the area of language or vocabulary development. They also could be confused by information that differs or is absent from their personal background experiences. Provide extra scaffolding in any of these areas as needed.

FIGURE 6.4. Informal Assessment for Intermediate Readers and Writers

Assessment	How It Is Done	What to Look for in Students	If Students Need Additional Help in This Area
Vocabulary	Frequently check to see whether students know the meanings of important words used in the classroom. Ask them to use these words in group discussions or their writing reflections as they engage with the ideas and information in their texts.	Note whether students are not yet using key content vocabulary words in their discussions or writing. Notice the behaviors students use when they do not know the meaning of a word. Do they use reference materials, ask someone, or simply skip ahead?	Work explicitly with five to seven of the most important words in each literacy or content lesson. Provide many visuals to help students learn the meanings of words in their content studies. Develop graphic organizers such as semantic maps to help students learn the depth of meaning for important content words. Provide students with strategies for taking apart words to get at their possible meanings.
Developmental spelling	Ask students to spell a set of words that contain progressively more difficult features, for example, words with inflected endings affixed to Greek or Latin word roots (see Bear et al., 2012).	Note the features that students use correctly such as doubling consonants (e.g., drumming) or dropping the e before adding –ing (e.g., skating). When students make attempts that are not always correct, that pinpoints where word study instruction should begin.	Students' spelling samples tell you where you need to begin instruction. Find the word study activities that practice the spelling processes that students are "using but confusing."

Assessment	How It Is Done	What to Look for in Students	If Students Need Additional Help in This Area
Writing	After reading widely in a particular genre, and analyzing this same type of writing with students, guide students to write their own piece. Allow students to proceed through the writing process, but have them save each draft to show their revisions.	Depending on the genre under study, look for students' coherent idea development, language use, word choice, and voice (see Pinnell & Fountas, 2007). Look for students to use evidence, choose domain-specific vocabulary, use dialogue, and establish a structure for their text, including a conclusion. Reviewing previous drafts of writing should demonstrate students' improvement in the goals listed above.	Students who have difficulty adhering to the features of a particular genre may need more explicit outlines or frame sentences to structure their writing. A thesaurus or other reference materials can support the use of more descriptive or precise language. Graphic organizers can help students think through and elaborate on their writing ideas. Peer writing groups also may provide encouragement and new ideas.
Reading comprehension	After students have read a section of text, ask them to discuss the material or make a prediction about what may happen next. Students also can retell or write a summary of their reading.	Look for accurate or reasonable predictions. Students also should be able to describe characters and events and discuss literary themes. Students who summarize the passage should be able to refer to details and main ideas, and describe the overall structure of information in a text.	Students who have difficulty with reading comprehension may need extra support in the area of language or vocabulary development. They also could be confused by information that differs or is absent from their personal background experiences, or by deeper themes that lie below the surface. Provide extra scaffolding in any of these areas as needed.

CHAPTER 7

Integrating Vocabulary and Academic Language Instruction with Reading and Writing Activities

I N PREVIOUS CHAPTERS of this book, I have stressed the importance of building language development opportunities into the school day. In Chapter 3 I discussed the value of focused English language development lessons for students who are still developing proficiency in oral English. These lessons build on students' growing oral and written skills in their new language and target specific areas of the language that tend to give learners difficulty, such as increasingly complex vocabulary, syntax, and pragmatic features. Language is clearly at the heart of every aspect of an engaging multilingual classroom.

This chapter takes a look at language instruction through another lens: The language demands that the reading and writing activities that occur each day in elementary classrooms place on students' vocabulary and academic language knowledge. I also investigate how teachers can build students' vocabulary and academic language while they conduct reading and writing lessons. The research tells us that a separate block of time for English language development is important (Saunders, Foorman, & Carlson, 2006), but we also know that many students need language scaffolding to access grade-level, standards-based material throughout the day. I offer ideas for a set of teaching habits that integrate language instruction into literacy lessons by:

1. assessing student background knowledge
2. identifying the academic language demands of texts and other materials, including key vocabulary words
3. creating language models that build students' vocabulary and syntactical knowledge
4. engaging in conversations in which students refine their ability to use new vocabulary and academic language in context

In the second half of this chapter, I present three vignettes of reading and writing lessons that highlight the use of teaching strategies to build academic language.

BUILDING VOCABULARY INTO LITERACY LESSONS

Before launching into the teaching process for developing academic language, I present a few quick tips for including vocabulary into any literacy activities going on in your classroom. The following lists of dos and don'ts outline some of the things you might keep in mind as you enrich your curriculum with vocabulary study (Helman, 2008). As you read the lists, reflect on your areas of strength as a teacher of content or general academic vocabulary, and determine what additional support you might need. In which areas would you like to seek out additional information?

Dos in Vocabulary Instruction

SELECT IMPORTANT WORDS. There are so many interesting and unknown words in students' materials that teachers could spend all of their time in class on vocabulary instruction. In each lesson, select the most critical three to seven words to teach. Ask yourself, "What words are essential to my students' understanding of the key concepts in this material?" For instance, in a writing lesson involving the creation of opinion pieces, key words likely would include *opinion*, *reason*, and *convince*.

BUILD ON WHAT STUDENTS KNOW. To find out what students know about a subject, use discussion, questioning, exit tickets, or group projects in which each individual contributes a piece. Then, connect the content that students are familiar with to bridge to the new learning material. For example, when studying fables, a teacher might ask students to talk with their families about a story that taught a lesson or had a moral. In class, students could draw a character from their story and add it to a class bulletin board. The teacher is now able to connect new vocabulary to the words students have been sharing.

MAKE SURE STUDENTS TELL YOU WHEN THEY DON'T UNDERSTAND. Many students will be shy about speaking up in class when they don't know something, such as the meaning of a word. When students don't share their questions, teachers lose a teaching opportunity and students likely will miss out on the learning goal of the lesson. Make it a norm in your classroom that students self-monitor their understanding of the words being presented and are praised for asking questions. Set up procedures for whom to ask when important, unknown words come up.

PRESENT WORDS IN A MEANINGFUL CONTEXT. When an unknown word arises, find a way to use the word in a child-friendly sentence, act it out, or show a picture that clarifies the word. Students likely will not learn a word if they are given only a verbal definition that goes by quickly. One way teachers can clarify is to have a computer and projector ready in the classroom for looking up images of vocabulary words and projecting them on the wall for students to see during lessons.

CONNECT TO STUDENTS' HOME LANGUAGES AND COGNATES. Begin to investigate your students' home languages to find out whether cognates exist. Or, ask students whether their language has a similar word to the one you are discussing. This creates a sense of word curiosity in the classroom and also creates support for multilingual diversity. For example, when encountering the word *congratulate* in a read-aloud text, the teacher asks, "How do you say that in your home language?"

BUILD ON WORD-LEARNING STRATEGIES. Use opportunities that arise in content area lessons such as science, math, or social studies to make connections to the word-learning skills you are addressing during word study time. After identifying some unknown and important words in the content, reinforce the phonics skills they contain or notice the patterns in homophonic words, or take apart affixes and roots in longer words. For example, a teacher might model how to take apart *photosynthesis* and ask, "What other words do you know that have *photo* in them?"

DEVELOP AN ATMOSPHERE THAT SUPPORTS WORD CONSCIOUSNESS. Get excited about learning new words and compliment students when they make connections among words. Display artifacts in class, such as lists of favorite words, descriptive words, scary words, funny words, and so on.

Don'ts in Vocabulary Instruction

DON'T ASSUME THAT ALL STUDENTS KNOW AND CAN USE ALL COMMON VO-CABULARY WORDS. Depending on students' previous schooling and language experiences, they may have gaps in the words in their personal lexicon. It is always good to check for understanding even with basic words.

DON'T GO ON EXTENDED "BIRDWALKS" TO CONVERSE ABOUT PARTICULAR WORDS. Vocabulary conversations can take away time from other important content studies. Keep discussions concise and comprehensible. Have extended conversations about words, and the stories that go with them, during noninstructional times such as while waiting in the lunch line.

DON'T FOCUS ON EXOTIC OR "BOUTIQUE" WORDS. Students will need many experiences with a word to remember it and be able to use it in their oral and written language. Avoid spending a lot of time on words that students are not likely to encounter often.

DON'T ASK STUDENTS TO COPY WORDS MULTIPLE TIMES OR LOOK THEM UP IN THE DICTIONARY. These activities are not productive for learning new words in elementary school, and they tend to take a lot of time away from more important learning. Until students have learned the mechanics of dictionary use in the upper grades and until they have access to dictionaries that are simple enough for them to learn the meanings of words, they should not be expected to look up words in the dictionary.

DON'T EXPECT STUDENTS TO COMPLETELY UNDERSTAND OR REMEMBER A WORD AFTER ONLY ONE EXPOSURE. It takes numerous contacts in a variety of settings for students to begin to have a new word at their disposal. Structure opportunities for students to hear, discuss, read, and use important words over and over.

THE LANGUAGE DEMANDS OF READING AND WRITING ACTIVITIES

Most teachers have had the experience of preparing an exciting lesson only to find that their students were not able to complete the activity successfully. Perhaps there was a writing structure students were not yet familiar with, or maybe the task simply had too many steps for the students to juggle. Teachers learn from these less-than-successful activities. They may realize they need to take a step back to scaffold the lesson better, or they might decide that the content is beyond the reach of students at this point in time. In fact, one reason students may struggle with tasks at school may be the overload of academic English demands.

The Complexity of Academic English Proficiency

Scarcella (2003) describes academic English proficiency as having three parts: a linguistic dimension, a cognitive dimension, and a sociocultural/psychological dimension. The linguistic dimension relates to the sounds, words, grammar, and pragmatics of language use, as described in Chapter 3 of this book. The cognitive dimension involves thinking skills and using background knowledge in a task. Finally, the sociocultural/psychological dimension of academic English relates to the social application of the literacy practices. For example, if a task involved knowing how to write an invitation, a student would need to know not only the technical aspects of writing, but also why and how invitations are shared in certain cultural settings (Brock, Lapp, Salas, & Townsend, 2009; Scarcella, 2003).

Each academic task at school involves demands on students' linguistic, cognitive, and sociocultural resources. When those demands go unexamined, responsibility for succeeding or failing on projects is assigned to students. To help all students find success, it is useful to deconstruct the academic language demands of lessons and assignments to clarify the linguistic, cognitive, and sociocultural resources that are required.

Identifying Language Demands

With each lesson or assignment at school, consider what students will need to know and be able to do to complete it accurately and comprehensively. What receptive skills (e.g., listening or reading) or productive skills (e.g., speaking or writing) will students be using (Performance Assessment for California Teachers, 2010)? Analyze each step of the lesson to clearly identify linguistic, cognitive, or sociocultural knowledge students will need. The list below provides a beginning idea of what to consider.

- Listening. For how long and at what oral comprehension level will students need to be able to process information? What is the key collection of vocabulary words that will be necessary to process the content information? What general academic vocabulary (e.g., summary, represent) will be needed to understand processes or directions? What participation norms do students need to follow to learn effectively from listening?
- Speaking. Will students need to answer questions in a large or small group or have a discussion with a partner? Will they need to present or share information to be successful? What expectations are there for taking turns and participating?
- Reading. What is the approximate reading level of any texts involved in the lesson? What background knowledge or experiences with genres and text structures (e.g., graphic novel, folktale, chronology, cause/effect) will be needed? What grammatical/syntactical structures are embedded in the language of the text? What textual

resources such as headings, tables, graphics, and so on, will students need to understand? What processes such as comprehensive reading or skimming will students need to call on to be efficient in the task? What metacognitive skills or reading comprehension strategies will likely be needed?

- Writing. How much and at what level of proficiency will students need to be able to write in order to be successful? What vocabulary will they need to come up with on their own? Will they need to understand simple or elaborate argument structures or specific text structures (e.g., informative, narrative, opinion) in the task? Does the genre require use of any special features such as connector words, grammatical structures (e.g., the passive voice), or text organization strategies (Performance Assessment for California Teachers, 2010)? What writing strategies (e.g., planning with a graphic organizer, drafting, revising) will be useful to completing the project?

INTEGRATING ACADEMIC LANGUAGE INSTRUCTION INTO LITERACY LESSONS

There is not enough time in the day for teachers to have separate instruction in all of the academic language skills that students require. Most of the language teaching that happens will need to take place in the context of standards-based lessons within the content areas. So, teachers need techniques for integrating vocabulary, the sound system, complex language structures, and pragmatic knowledge about language use into their daily lessons. In this section, I outline four steps in a process for doing this, including assessing student background knowledge, identifying the academic language demands of the task, creating models and demonstrations to support student learning, and engaging in conversations and guided practice with students.

Assess Student Background Knowledge

Chapter 6 in this book outlined informal assessments for better understanding students' language and literacy capabilities. Use these as well as content-based tasks (e.g., field notes in a science journal or the student's latest creative writing project) to gain an awareness of where students are before launching into a new area of study or assignment with them. Informal assessments may be as simple as a K-W-L chart (Ogle, 1986) or a small-group discussion about a topic. Keep a notepad or checklist at hand to jot down what you are learning about individual students and their background knowledge. If most of the students in your class have limited experiences with a particular topic, skill, strategy, or cluster of vocabulary words, it may be a sign to take the academic plans slowly and provide a lot of scaffolding. If you find that only a handful of students have limited background knowledge of the topic, you likely will want to find ways for them to learn from the experiences of others in the group.

Identify the Academic Language Demands of the Task

Review the list of questions presented earlier in this chapter to identify the listening, speaking, reading, and writing demands of a task. Consider the linguistic, cognitive, and sociocultural components of the directions, content, skills, and social expectations included in the lesson. After you have analyzed the academic requirements, go back to your student assessments and ask: In what areas will students need support to be successful? Chart the academic language demands on one side of a sheet of paper and note areas for student support on the other side.

Create Models to Support Student Learning

Students may require support in one or more areas of academic language on a given task. For social demands such as working with a partner or in a small group and following a set of steps in a collaborative learning activity, teachers often model and have students practice the behaviors in a whole-group setting ahead of time. For learning about complex syntactical structures within particular reading or writing genres, a mini-lesson on text features may be more appropriate. Figure 7.1 outlines some of the ways models might be created to help students learn academic English.

Later in this chapter I present three specific examples of how teachers have analyzed the language demands of their literacy activities and then applied models such as those presented in Figure 7.1.

Engage in Conversations and Guided Practice with Students

Once models have been created for students to reference, the next step in teaching is to discuss them and have students create their own versions with guided support and feedback. For example, after creating a list of related vocabulary words, students might participate in guessing games about the words such as, "I am thinking of a word that _____." Then, they could write or tell simple stories using the content vocabulary words. After reviewing characteristics of a particular text genre, such as poetry, poems are read and compared with the features that had been noted on the class chart. Students use content vocabulary such *rhythm, rhyme,* or *verse* to discuss aspects of the genre. Conversations like these give teachers the opportunity to hear students' confusions about the models being studied and give feedback. Following this step, students create their own example of what is being studied using the models and with explicit help from the teacher. When possible, steps are outlined on procedure charts for student reference. As students produce verbal or written products, this again provides an opportunity for teachers to identify areas of linguistic, cognitive, or sociocultural challenges that need to be supported.

FIGURE 7.1. Tasks and Possible Models for Teaching Academic English

Type of Language Demand	Possible Models to Guide Students
Content vocabulary	Vocabulary is organized around a cohesive concept related to the theme (e.g., magnetism, fantasy texts, writing a newspaper). Relevant vocabulary is posted, with photo clues, on vocabulary word walls and class charts.
Procedural or general academic vocabulary	Lists of relevant vocabulary such as *summarize, analyze, retell, group, identify, share,* and so on, are posted, explained, and practiced in small- and large-group contexts.
Syntactic structures in text	After the teacher has identified the kinds of sentences used in reading texts or called for in writing texts, frame sentences and sentence construction charts are designed for reference and practice (Dutro & Helman, 2009). Representative sentences are posted and analyzed for students to review as needed.
Use of connector words that influence sentence meaning	Based on the text structures and genres being studied, chart lists of connector words (e.g., *because, first, then, however, instead*) are posted and/or provided to students for their writing notebooks. As new connector words are found in grade-level texts, they are discussed, defined, and added to the charts or lists for reference.
Features of particular genres of texts	Charts or student handouts outline in simplified form the conventions that each genre typically uses. Lists of important vocabulary often used in each genre are included.
Metacognitive strategies to improve listening or speaking participation	Clear expectations are set for what active listening and active group participation look like in the classroom. Procedure charts are developed to remind students about these behaviors. Teachers take time to think out loud about the things taking place in their head while listening or speaking in a class discussion. Students are asked to reflect on their participation and learning from group or partner discussions.
Social language and behaviors for collaborative engagement	Clear expectations are set for language use, participation, and turn taking when working in small groups. Procedure charts are developed to remind students about these behaviors. Lists of helpful language for groupwork are posted and referenced regularly. Small groups of students demonstrate the collaborative behaviors for the class (fishbowl) as a way to discuss what meaningful interaction looks like and sounds like.
Reading skills or strategies	When texts are beyond students' decoding or comprehension levels, scaffolds are put in place to give them access to the material (e.g., recorded versions, translated versions, modified language versions, shared reading with teachers). Comprehension strategies are posted in the classroom and referenced at the moment of need in reading tasks.
Writing skills or strategies	Examples of sentences and mentor texts are posted for students to work from. Students are provided with a variety of graphic organizers to help structure their writing plan. Words that may be useful to particular writing genres are posted or are collaboratively created with students for their writing notebooks. When writing demands are beyond students' developmental spelling levels, students write as much as they can on their own and dictate the rest.

After engaging in the discussion and guided practice steps, teachers should know whether students are ready to handle the academic task independently. Teachers look for students to demonstrate the vocabulary, sentence structures, textual features, and social interaction skills represented in the content under study.

EXAMPLES OF ACADEMIC LANGUAGE SUPPORT AT VARIOUS GRADE LEVELS

In the final section of this chapter I share examples of how three teachers provided scaffolds for academic language learning during literacy instruction with their multilingual students. Phil is a first-grade teacher, Beth is a third-grade teacher, and Elena is a fifth-grade teacher. Each of the teachers demonstrates how to assess student background knowledge, uses models for student reference, engages in guided conversations and practice, and provides explicit feedback to increase students' academic language development.

A First-Grade Phonics Lesson

In Phil's first-grade classroom, students bring a variety of home language background experiences. Students are doing well on grade-level benchmarks for phonics skills in English such as letter–sound correspondences, and a good number of students are beginning to ask about and try out spelling using consonant digraphs such as *ch, sh,* and *th* in their developmental spelling. Before working with students on this academic task, Phil asks himself about the language challenges his students might face in this area. Figure 7.2 outlines some of what Phil considers as he reflects on the upcoming lesson.

Because Phil has thought carefully about the phonics task he will be presenting to students, he is better prepared to scaffold their academic language learning. Before he begins the digraph study, he introduces and plays guessing games using words that begin with the focus sounds. He also adds digraphs and key pictures to the alphabet cards throughout the room. By his doing these two things, students begin to use more words orally that begin with digraphs, and Phil notices any pronunciation issues that come up for students. In fact, Phil notices that students from Spanish-speaking backgrounds sometimes confuse the /sh/ and /ch/ sounds. He decides to start the phonics lesson using only /ch/ and /th/ and to add /sh/ later. Finally, Phil takes the time to discuss, model, and practice how to do a word sort with a partner before expecting students to do that on their own.

A Third-Grade Reading Lesson

Beth's third-grade students bring a range of language and literacy resources with them to the classroom. Some students are recent immigrants from war-torn countries who are beginning speakers of English and reading one to two grade levels below district expectations. Other students are meeting or exceeding many benchmark standards but have the most difficulty with academic vocabulary and complex language structures. The lesson she is preparing involves a third-grade reading standard for

FIGURE 7.2. Identifying Academic Language Requirements and Support Needed in a First-Grade Classroom

	Studying Consonant Digraphs at the Beginning of Words	**Ideas for Creating Models to Support Student Learning**
Linguistic demands	Do students have a good supply of vocabulary words in their oral language that start with *ch, sh*, and *th*? Do the digraphs represent sounds that are difficult for students from particular language backgrounds to pronounce or distinguish?	Introduce a set of common picture cards that begin with *ch, sh*, or *th* for vocabulary study prior to doing the lesson. Listen to students talk and scan their unedited writing—do they confuse any of these English sounds? If so, begin with digraphs that are less confusing.
Cognitive demands	Can students associate single letters with the sounds they represent? Do students' informal literacy assessments demonstrate that they are ready to work on this literacy skill?	Post, near the alphabet chart in the classroom, a digraph chart that shows a common key word for each digraph sound. Provide students with a personal alphabet page that has an addendum with each of the digraphs and a key word.
Sociocultural demands	Are students able to speak up in small-group lessons and take turns as they sort or play games with partners?	Create, in collaboration with students, a set of partner work procedures and discuss them in a class meeting. Have several sets of students demonstrate responsible behaviors for partner time.

distinguishing literal from nonliteral language in texts. Before Beth plans her lesson, she considers how to gather information about students' background knowledge in this area. She decides to create several figurative (nonliteral) statements and several concrete (literal) statements to see whether students can tell them apart. Next she will see whether students can think of a literal or nonliteral statement on their own. Beth writes, "Time flew by" and "The duck flew by" to use as header cards. She then brainstorms six other phrases to use with students that represent literal or nonliteral language.

When Beth does the introductory lesson with students, she finds that many, but not all, are able to sort the phrases into categories she calls "true" or "creative." She is now ready to think about the academic language demands of the upcoming lesson and plan models for student support. Figure 7.3 outlines some of her thinking as she plans.

After planning, Beth meets with the small group of students who need additional support. She writes down the literal and nonliteral phrases from her work with that group to use again in the large group.

Now Beth is ready for the modeled mini-lesson. She demonstrates and discusses the concepts of literal and nonliteral language and introduces the key vocabulary in child-friendly language, connecting the word *literal* to the phrase "is that *literally* true?" She asks students to take out their independent reading texts and reread them, looking for examples of literal and nonliteral language. During this guided activity Beth checks student work and provides feedback as needed. After 5 minutes students

FIGURE 7.3. Identifying Academic Language Requirements and Support Needed in a Third-Grade Classroom

	Studying Literal and Nonliteral Language	**Ideas for Creating Models to Support Student Learning**
Linguistic demands	The lesson will include some conceptual content vocabulary words such as *literal, nonliteral, literally,* and *figure of speech.* There are likely to be a number of unknown vocabulary words present in the literal and nonliteral examples pulled from the stories that the class examines. Third-grade reading texts use increasingly complex sentence structures. The focus sentence structure for the lesson will be, "It is very creative to say _____, but not literally true."	Create a chart with a line down the middle to start collecting literal and nonliteral phrases. As the chart develops, ask students to illustrate the phrases. It is not realistic to predict every unknown vocabulary word that may arise in the lesson, so Beth titles a blank piece of chart paper, "Interesting words we found." Write the frame sentence on pocket chart cards (see Figure 7.4). Have extra cards available to write in the nonliteral phrases that students find.
Cognitive demands	The material students will examine comes from leveled readers that should be accessible to each student. The challenge will be to support students who were not entirely successful in the introductory (pre-assessment) lesson.	Beth decides to provide an additional explicit lesson for the five students who had difficulty with the concept in the introductory lesson. During the lesson she will help them find phrases to present to the class later.
Sociocultural demands	Students will need to be able to work in groups to share their literal and nonliteral phrases. Students will use social language that helps their peers know whether they are on the right track in their pursuit of sample phrases.	Pull out and practice the "Working in Groups" procedure chart the class has used before. Brainstorm with the group a list of polite sentence starters that may be used to give the people in a group feedback such as, "You found _____. Nice job!" "Here's a suggestion . . . ," "You might try . . . ," "Tell me more about . . . ."

volunteer to share their language samples, and Beth writes some of the phrases on the pocket chart cards, an easy way to manipulate word or picture cards into groups or sentences. Figure 7.4 shows students working collaboratively at a pocket chart (c.f., Bear, Helman & Woessner, 2009). Students reread the sentences as a group; for example, "It is very creative to say *he lost his head*, but it's not literally true."

Following the modeled mini-lesson and guided practice, students are now ready to work on their own in small groups. The class reviews procedures for small-group work and brainstorms things that would be good to

FIGURE 7.4. Children Engaged with a Pocket Chart

say to a peer to provide feedback. Beth has done many things to support the academic language learning of her group of third graders.

A Fifth-Grade Reading/Writing Lesson

Elena's classroom community is lively and interested in everything. Students' desks are crammed with reading materials of many kinds, as well as with writer's notebooks, textbooks, and composition books for each subject. Her students read at levels from second to seventh grade, and they come from four home language groups, including English. The lesson that Elena is planning today is based on a fifth-grade text titled, "Ultimate Field Trip 5: Blasting Off to Space Academy" (Goodman, 2001). The standard she will address involves explaining the relationships or interactions between two or more individuals in a scientific text based on specific information in the text (Council of Chief State School Officers, 2010).

To get an idea of her students' background knowledge, Elena asks each student to create a simple graphic organizer using circles and lines to show who the people are in the student's current independent reading book and how they relate. If the book has a lot of people, students should pick no more than four to include in their graphic organizer. The goal is to show how the people in the text are connected to one another and what kinds of interactions they have.

When Elena collects students' papers, she sees a wide variation in their understanding of the relationships within the texts. Some students

FIGURE 7.5. Overview of Fifth-Grade Reading and Writing Lesson
with Instructional Supports

Lesson Component	Additional Support Provided
Preview important content and general academic vocabulary.	Use of visuals and kid-friendly definitions. Words are posted on charts for reference.
Discuss two-part quotations as a sentence structure.	Students have a handout of examples for reference.
Read the text independently or in a guided group with the teacher.	Teacher supports below-grade-level students in a guided lesson.
In partnerships or in a teacher-guided group, identify places where a person's role is clarified by a short phrase before or after the name (appositive).	Examples are provided initially to students.
Model a graphic organizer of the people in the space academy text.	Modeling of process students will be doing.
Individuals go back to their previously submitted graphic organizers to see whether they want to change anything before resubmitting them.	Students build on previous work. Examples of graphic organizers are provided.

have lines connecting each person to everyone else, while others seem
to show each person as a separate and isolated individual. Elena thinks
the following areas will be important for developing students' academic
English in this lesson:

1. *Content vocabulary*. Key words, including *gravity*, *environment*,
   astronaut, *mission*, *weightless*, *academy*.
2. *General academic vocabulary*. The words *relationship*, *interaction*,
   function, *simulate*.
3. *Syntactical structure*. Two-part quotations such as, "I don't think so,"
   said David. "You wouldn't catch me doing that."
4. *Getting information from text*. Locating specific information about
   people's relationships based on how they are introduced in the text.
5. *Writing*. Producing an evidence-based graphic organizer that
   conceptually outlines relationships within a text.

She plans to use the following models to support students' learning in
each area:

1. Find images of the content words on the web (e.g., *weightless*) to
   present to students to clarify the word's meaning.
2. Put general academic vocabulary on a piece of chart paper to be
   reviewed. Kid-friendly definitions and sentences will help clarify the
   meanings of words.

3. Select several examples of two-part quotations from the reading text and type them onto a handout for students to review and discuss.

4. Identify spots in the text where a person's role or relationship is clarified through an appositive such as, "the principal, who is the leader of the school, ..."

5. Provide examples of radial graphic organizers for students to consider as they rewrite their evidence-based graphic organizers, and include quotations from people in the text.

Figure 7.5 presents an overview of the lesson that Elena conducted with her class using the grade-level text about the space academy.

In this lesson students had support for accessing grade-level material while being challenged to pursue high-level reading and writing standards.

SUMMARY

This chapter has outlined the pressing need for teachers to thoughtfully develop vocabulary and academic language with students throughout their language arts lessons. I described how teachers can examine the linguistic, cognitive, and sociocultural demands of specific language arts tasks assigned to students in class. Then, to better prepare students for success, teachers assess student background knowledge, provide models for student reference, engage students in guided conversations and practice, and communicate explicit feedback on their learning. This series of instructional steps paves the way for students to better understand the complex vocabulary and academic language structures they need in order to flourish.

CHAPTER 8

Creating Engaging Instruction in Multilingual Classrooms

T HE GOAL of this book is to present ways for teachers to learn about and engage with their multilingual elementary students for increased language and literacy learning. This is no small feat given that every day elementary classrooms become more and more complex, whether we consider the great variation in students' background experiences or the increased expectations for standards-based performance. In this chapter I review the breadth of topics outlined in the book and suggest ways to work with your students, their families, and your colleagues to put these ideas into action. This process is transformational, but should not feel frenzied. It is a way of coming together for students' growth.

I begin by sharing several overarching ideas about effective instruction for students from multilingual backgrounds. I frame effective instructional practices in four general areas: engaging in a learning community, explicit and systematic instruction, highlighting connections, and actively constructing new knowledge. I summarize the big ideas from chapters in this book and show how they lead to engaging learning for students, as well as enhanced family involvement. I present several examples of how effective teachers motivate, involve, and teach their diverse students by providing interaction, language support, and high expectations. At the end of the chapter I revisit the three overarching themes of this book—community, language-enriched literacy, and engagement. I argue that each of these big ideas is critical for student success and family participation. I provide suggested next steps for educators on their journeys forward in the profession.

EFFECTIVE INSTRUCTION FOR LANGUAGE LEARNERS

In a recent review of the literature Claude Goldenberg (in press) outlines what is known about instructional practices that best serve English learners. He outlines four big ideas:

1. Many teaching practices that have been found to be effective with students in general show a likelihood of being successful with English learners.
2. Students with limited English proficiency need modifications or increased instructional supports in class.
3. English learners need many opportunities and explicit instruction to develop proficiency in oral and written English.
4. Students' home languages are an important resource for building academic learning.

Research that has been conducted with linguistically diverse students generally substantiates one or more of the features of effective instruction in general, such as clear goals, procedures, and routines; modeling, practice, and feedback; active engagement and student interaction; and frequent informal assessment. I have been using a model over the past 10 years that consolidates many of these features of effective instruction, but with a lens on the specific strengths and challenges for English learners. This model clusters effective teaching strategies into four key areas: engaging in a learning community, explicit and systematic instruction, highlighting connections, and actively constructing new knowledge (Helman,

2009). Examples of strategies for scaffolding literacy instruction include providing embedded language and vocabulary development within lessons; making content comprehensible through the use of visuals and hands-on materials; moving from simple, guided activities to meaningful independent practice; and setting up structures for each member of the classroom learning community to interact and provide support to others. In the next section I describe these areas in more depth and connect them to the ideas from previous chapters.

Engaging in a Learning Community

We learn from and with one another. When students feel connected to their peers and teachers, and when families feel a part of the school community, the combined efforts of the school and its students and their families create a synergy that promotes student success. Student growth leads to more learning, and academic or social problems at school are addressed early on through communication. One of the ways teachers can encourage learning communities for students is to create a low-anxiety classroom environment where students work in small groups and are free to make mistakes and ask questions. Also, teachers can build individual relationships with students and make it clear that they expect each student's best efforts. Students should have opportunities to work together, get to know one another, and take responsibility for the whole group's progress. Procedures and classroom routines should be clearly stated and reinforced, and students should practice celebrating the diverse languages, cultures, and background experiences of their fellow students. The classroom learning community should resemble a family—students should know they will be missed when they are absent, listened to when they have a story to tell, and honored when they accomplish a milestone. The classroom community should be one where students want to come to school, and teachers should take pride and enjoyment in the progress they see every day.

This book has outlined dozens of ways for teachers and school leaders to develop community with the students and families they serve. Chapter 2 focused on many aspects of this process, from setting up the physical environment, to maintaining consistent routines and procedures, to upholding norms for respectful interactions. Central to building the collaborative spirit that makes classrooms places of engagement and learning is to bring students' experiences and family resources into instruction. Chapter 2 outlined ways to welcome, honor, and connect with parents around student learning. The chapter highlighted specific learning activities for incorporating families into the school community and showing students that their home languages and cultures are respected.

Foundational to engaging in a learning community is that members get to know and care about one another. Chapter 2 also had numerous suggestions for how teachers can build bonds with their students in easy, matter-of-fact ways. Teachers invest in their students' feelings of connection toward school each time they greet students with a smile, take the time for a private chat, or make an out-of-school connection. In addition, as teachers structure climates of respect and collaboration, students become key members of their classmates' successful learning. In all of the chapters of this book, the procedures and teaching practices presented reveal how classrooms can become shared spaces for individual and collective growth.

Explicit and Systematic Instruction

A number of teaching practices discussed in Goldenberg's (in press) review of the research on effective instruction concern the need for English learners to receive explicit and systematic instruction. Some elements of explicit instruction include giving clear input; modeling expectations; providing feedback to learners; using visuals, hands-on materials, and graphic organizers; and encouraging additional practice. Many of us have been in an unfamiliar and challenging setting, and we understand that learning often happens best when content is easy to understand and straightforward. Clear directions, explicit language, and keeping things as simple as possible can all be very helpful for learning. All elementary students, no matter what their language backgrounds, *profit* from clear teaching that is appropriate to their instructional level. Students who are challenged to understand the vocabulary or academic language of school *require* clear teaching that is appropriate to their developmental level if they are to be successful.

This book is replete with ideas for making instruction systematic and explicit. Some examples include posting routines and procedures for learning and transitional activities in class, and practicing those routines regularly. Chapter 3 makes a case for the importance of explicit and systematic English language development instruction for students who have yet to achieve proficiency. It is helpful for students when teachers provide regular English language development lessons that teach the vocabulary, grammar, syntax, and conventions of English. Academic language must be a focus, with specific language objectives outlined. Thus, teachers need a strong background in oral and written English so they understand the process of language growth for their developing students and can teach them the regularities of the language.

The chapters in this book that addressed student learning in reading, writing, and vocabulary highlighted many ways for teachers to provide explicit instruction. Sentence frames provide models for student writing. Material should be at students' instructional level, so that students always expect to be able to understand and keep up with the appropriately challenging work. The instructional level should be determined by ongoing, informal assessment by the classroom teacher. A process of modeling, then guiding, and finally having students practice independently (i.e., I do, we do, you do) is key to effective, explicit, and systematic instruction.

Highlighting Connections

New learning builds on previous knowledge for young and old alike. One key component of effective instruction is that it links to the learner's background knowledge. Highlighting connections means helping students see how what they are learning relates to what they already know and, in turn, what this means in the real world. Key to providing effective literacy instruction for English learners is the ability to tailor lessons that build on what students know, while stretching them to grasp the classroom content. Teachers highlight connections when they show students how oral and written language are related. When links are made between skill instruction and meaningful reading and writing activities, students see the purpose of their literacy lessons. Each time teachers connect students' personal experiences and background knowledge to school activities, the goals for learning become clearer to students and they feel greater involvement in their education.

Another way to think about teachers who effectively highlight connections for their students is that they help the learner apply and transfer what is being learned to new situations. An example of this is when a student learns a new vocabulary word or sentence structure. Applying that language in a new setting for the first time would be showing "transfer."

Graphic organizers are an excellent tool to help students make connections. A symbolic representation such as a Venn diagram or concept map compels students to visualize the relationship between people, ideas, or things. When students cannot conceptualize what they are learning, it is a hint that teachers need to give additional practice or engage in learning conversations.

Many examples of how to highlight connections were presented in this book. First and foremost, there were extensive ideas for connecting what students bring from home to their new learning at school. At every possible opportunity, teachers are encouraged to interact with students about their home languages and experiences. Students are invited to share the connections they see in storytelling, reading, writing, and the meaning of words used at home and in school. Books, alphabets, artifacts, poems, and songs from many languages are shared in class. Students are encouraged to write and read in a home language if it helps them develop proficiency and content knowledge in their new language. Assessment of students' literacy skills in their home language informs teachers about how to best help them progress.

A key component for integrating academic language instruction into literacy lessons is outlined in Chapter 7. In this four-step process, the first step is to assess background knowledge. It is critical for teachers to understand where to begin with students before designing and implementing the teaching plan.

Actively Constructing New Knowledge

We learn by doing and by solving problems. Effective teachers know that the best learning comes when students experience challenging, yet doable, tasks and are asked to actively participate. Uribe and Nathenson-Mejía (2008) describe a structure for lessons aimed at new speakers of English: Day 1, Build On; Day 2, Explain and Involve; Day 3, Explain and Involve; Day 4, Involve; Day 5, Involve. Some of the ways that students can actively construct new knowledge are by working with hands-on materials, using their bodies, playing games, doing authentic tasks, and having time to interact in conversations with teachers and peers around content.

Students who are learning a new culture and language at school profit from doing tasks that have authentic meaning outside of the classroom. For example, writing and delivering a message have a clear purpose in the world. On the other hand, responding to a writing prompt in a class journal does not carry the same contextualized meaning and students might need more of a rationale for why they are doing it. Wise teachers find ways to teach subject matter by getting students to actively participate in material of great interest to them personally (Harvey & Daniels, 2009).

How has actively constructing new knowledge been featured in this book? Parents are invited to share what authentic learning looks like in the student's home. This information helps teachers create hybrid events at school that engage students in ways that make sense to them (Au, 2009). Informal assessments help pinpoint the "just right" level for literacy instruction so that students are challenged. In ELD lessons students examine the words, sentences, and texts at their oral language proficiency level to make sense of the complexity of the English language. Students are encouraged to write in "the best way they can" as they express their daily experiences, ideas, and new learning. In literacy lessons students first see a model, then practice with guidance, and finally have opportunities to engage in learning activities with partners and independently. All of these lesson formats encourage active engagement in new learning.

EFFECTIVE TEACHERS ORCHESTRATE A LANGUAGE-LEARNING CLASSROOM

In this chapter I describe in detail what effective instruction looks like and how it is experienced from a student perspective. It's important to keep in mind that behind every smoothly running, actively engaged classroom of students is one key person: the teacher. Teachers organize the classroom environment, assess student learning, and plan appropriate learning activities. Teachers set the climate for cooperation and mutual support, and they help each student to feel safe and challenged. Without the teacher there cannot be an engaging multilingual learning community.

Michael Graves (2006) describes the language-filled classroom of a fourth-grade teacher who finds success by "providing rich and varied language experiences, teaching individual words, teaching word-learning strategies, and fostering word consciousness" (p. 145). So much of the learning that happens within a classroom depends on the orchestration of the classroom leader—the teacher.

Effective teachers are very cognizant of the role that language plays in the classroom. They are aware that students who are verbal and articulate in the academic language of the classroom tend to speak up more and may monopolize classroom "air time." For this reason, effective teachers use many of the techniques outlined in this book to make the language of the classroom accessible to all students. Effective teachers also create a variety of ways for students to participate—in partnerships, in small groups, and in one-on-one conferences with the teacher.

EFFECTIVE TEACHERS COLLABORATE WITH STUDENTS, PARENTS, AND COLLEAGUES

Teachers have a central role in the classroom, but they will not be successful if they try to do everything by themselves. Many teachers face burnout as they try to shoulder the weight of the world on their back and be the best teacher possible. Teaching is a physically and mentally demanding job in which many decisions are made every hour. By the end of the teaching day, there is little energy left.

I suggest that the most effective teacher (and one that will survive in the profession!) is the person who knows how to include others as team members. The teacher's first partners in the classroom are the students. Students want to help and be included. They show pride when given responsibility and learn from the leadership roles they take on. For this reason, investing in teacher-to-student and student-to-student relationships is critical each year in the classroom. Once these bonds have been created, students are the teacher's most plentiful and helpful collaborators.

As I have discussed throughout this book, another source of strength and collaboration for teachers is the students' family members. Some parents are available to be present at school regularly or from time to time. Others can participate by sending in notes or by supporting the school program through their actions and conversations with children at home. No matter what their time schedule permits, when family members are included as allies for student learning, everyone feels the load lifting. Try out the examples of strategies in this book to see whether involving family members to a greater degree changes your perspective on the stressfulness of teaching.

Many teachers find support and greater productivity by collaborating with colleagues. Various models exist for this cooperation, including collaboration among grade-level teams, vertical teams (e.g., second/

third/fourth-grade group), ELL and general education teachers, university–classroom partnerships, educational assistant and classroom teacher teams, or school-wide teaming to create focused instructional blocks of teaching. The benefits of collaboration are plentiful: It increases the knowledge of teaching and/or subject matter by adding expertise to one teacher's experience; it helps to differentiate instruction; it helps teachers have someone with whom to share ideas to improve instruction; and it provides another perspective about what individual students need in order to be successful. Reflection on teaching practice is a key element of continuous learning. When teachers collaborate to promote student success, it is more likely that authentic professional development will occur for team members.

PUTTING IT ALL TOGETHER

Three big concepts have pervaded this book: *community, literacy,* and *engagement.* Taken one at a time, each concept holds power for shaping the elementary school classroom. Building community makes teaching effective and learning powerful. It helps family members to contribute to their child's learning and influence the school program. Literacy is the key to learning in numerous disciplines. It is the end goal of much of what we strive for in schools. Engagement is how people and ideas interact and propel new learning. Without engagement we stay still. Engagement is the spark.

Teachers facilitate all three of these ideas each day in their multilingual classroom settings. They develop a *community* of *literacy* learners. They help students *engage* in *literacy.* With luck, teachers also *engage* their school *communities* in powerful *literacy* events and interactions.

This book began with my reflections on Carrie, a third-grade teacher in a diverse urban school. Carrie uses many of the strategies in this book in her teaching, yet she never quite feels accomplished enough to meet her own standards. When I talk to Carrie and other teachers like her, I encourage them to keep challenging themselves and learning from the students and communities with whom they work. We talk about how hard teaching is, but also about how much we learn from the community of learners we interact with every day. We are thrilled to know that tomorrow and the next day we will continue to have opportunities to engage in literacy-learning communities with our students.

After spending time with this book, it is my hope that you have connected the examples here with the effective teaching practices you already use and have been challenged by some new ideas to try out. I wish you the best in your continuing professional journey side-by-side with the students and families in your community.

Resources

ERE YOU WILL find important resources to help you put the ideas of this book into action. The selected resources are organized into six big areas: academic standards, assessment, family and community involvement, multilingual and multicultural resources, planning scaffolded instruction, and professional development. In each subsection I present links to organizations, materials, position papers, teaching tips, or other sites that will support your literacy instruction within engaging learning communities.

Academic Standards

The WIDA English Language Development (ELD) Standards outline the progression of English language development and describe how to teach academic language within the context of content-area instruction. These standards have been adopted by a majority of states: http://www.wida.us/standards/elp.aspx/.

The National Clearinghouse for English Language Acquisition (NCELA) provides resources about language and content-area standards: http://www.ncela.gwu.edu/assessment/.

The Common Core State Standards define the knowledge and skills students should develop within their K–12 education careers. The document entitled *Application of the Standards for English Language Learners* provides guidance on applying these standards with English learners: http://www.corestandards.org/the-standards/.

Assessment

Colorín Colorado has an ELL Starter Kit for Educators that provides helpful informal assessment forms for PK–12 educators who work with ELL students: http://www.colorincolorado.org/guides/sampler/.

Family and Community Involvement

Resource materials for families, including guides and reading tip sheets for parents of babies through elementary-aged students, are available in 11 languages from Colorín Colorado: www.colorincolorado.org/guides/readingtips/.

The Collaborative for Academic, Social, and Emotional Learning has many ideas for working with families and a packet of ideas and tools in English and Spanish: http://casel.org/publications/sel-parent-packet-ideas-and-tools-for-working-with-parents-and-families-full-packet/

The May 2011 special issue of *Educational Leadership* published by the Association for Supervision and Curriculum Development (ASCD) is devoted to schools, families, and communities.

The Minnesota Humanities Center provides tips for reading with children in 25 languages as well as several multicultural family reading programs: http://minnesotahumanities.org/resources/tips

Multilingual and Multicultural Resources

Background Information on Immigrant Populations

Energy of a Nation is the online immigration resource center of The Advocates for Human Rights, providing accurate, up-to-date information and resources for educators, advocates, and community members: http://www.energyofanation.org/.

Languages

The Alliance for the Advancement of Heritage Languages provides access to publications, newsletters, a database, and a listserv: http://www.cal.org/heritage/index.html/.

UCLA Language Materials Project provides teaching resources for less commonly taught languages: http://www.lmp.ucla.edu/.

Multilingual and Multicultural Literature

Barron's Educational Series has a wide selection of children's books in diverse languages. See www.barronseduc.com/children-s-books-foreign-languages-for-children.html/.

Benchmark Education publishes leveled books in English and Spanish that develop literacy, language, and content-area knowledge: www.benchmarkeducation.com/.

ChinaSprout offers books and resources for learning about Chinese culture and language: www.chinasprout.com/.

CincoPuntos Press features books in English and Spanish reflecting the culture of the American Southwest and Mexico: www.cincopuntos.com/

The International Children's Digital Library Foundation features scanned books in many languages: en.childrenslibrary.org/

Language Lizard sells bilingual and multicultural resource materials in over 40 languages at www.languagelizard.com

Master Communications offers materials and books that promote global understanding at http://www.master-comm.com/

Planning Instruction

The Metropolitan Center for Urban Education is a university-based center that targets issues related to educational equity by providing leadership and support to students, parents, teachers, administrators, and policymakers: http://steinhardt.nyu.edu/metrocenter/about/.

Responsive Classroom is a research-backed approach to elementary education that increases academic achievement, decreases problem behaviors, improves social skills, and leads to higher quality instruction: http://www.responsiveclassroom.org/.

Nonverbal Schools helps schools and organizations utilize nonverbal communication to improve classroom management: http://nonverbalclassroom.com/about/.

Pacific Education Group addresses educational inequity by providing guidance to districts as to how to meet the needs of underserved populations of students of color: http://www.pacificeducationalgroup.com/pages/home/.

Teaching Tolerance offers free teaching kits, such as Starting Small, a DVD and resource guide that profiles early-grade classrooms in which peace, equity, and justice are guiding themes: http://www.tolerance.org/teaching-kits/.

Principles for Scaffolded Instruction

The webinar "Effective Language Learning Strategies for English Language Learners" provides an overview of the CALLA framework for teaching language-learning strategies in the content and English-language-learning classroom: http://www.ncela.gwu.edu/webinars/event/16/.

Colorín Colorado For Educators is a repository for research, blogs, webinars, guides, and toolkits for teaching of English language learners: http://www.colorincolorado.org/educators/.

The SIOP Model

The Sheltered Instruction Observation Protocol (SIOP) Model was developed to facilitate high-quality instruction for English learners in content-area teaching: http://www.siopinstitute.net/.

Professional Development

Organizations and Position Papers

The American Federation of Teachers position paper on English language learners may be found at www.aft.org/newspubs/reports.

The American Speech-Language-Hearing Association offers multicultural resources for teaching and developing cultural competence at: www.asha.org/practice/multicultural/.

The ASCD provides links to numerous professional development resources connected to educating English learners: www.ascd.org/research-a-topic/english-language-learners-resources.aspx/.

AccELLerate! is NCELA's quarterly review, covering issues of interest to stakeholders in ELL education: http://www.ncela.gwu.edu/accellerate/.

NCELA also provides webinars of expert speakers presenting research on all aspects of ELL education: http://www.ncela.gwu.edu/webinars/.

The Center for Applied Linguistics (CAL) conducts projects and offers a variety of research-based resources related to the education of English language learners in a variety of settings: http://www.cal.org/topics/ell/.

References

Afflerbach, P. (2011). *Understanding and using reading assessment K–12.* Newark, DE: International Reading Association.

Allen, J. (2010). *Literacy in the welcoming classroom.* New York: Teachers College Press.

Anzaldúa, G. (1987). *Borderlands/La frontera: The new mestiza.* San Francisco: Aunt Lute Books.

Archambault, I., Eccles, J. S., & Vida, M. N. (2010). Ability self-concepts and subjective value in literacy: Joint trajectories from grades 1 through 12. *Journal of Educational Psychology, 102*(4), 804–816.

Au, K. (2009). Culturally responsive instruction: Application to multiethnic, multilingual classrooms. In L. Helman (Ed.), *Literacy development with English learners: Research-based instruction in grades K–6* (pp. 18–39). New York: Guilford Press.

Aud, S., Hussar, W., Planty, M., Snyder, T., Bianco, K., Fox, M., Frohlich, L., Kemp, J., & Drake, L. (2010). *The condition of education 2010* (NCES 2010-028). Washington, DC: National Center for Education Statistics, Institute of Education Sciences, U.S. Department of Education.

August, D., Goldenberg, C., Saunders, W. M., & Dressler, C. (2010). Recent research on English language and literacy instruction: What we have learned to guide practice for English language learners in the 21st century. In M. Shatz & L. C. Wilkinson (Eds.), *The education of English language learners: Research to practice* (pp. 272–297). New York: Guilford Press.

Bailey, A. L., & Heritage, M. (2008). *Formative assessment for literacy.* Thousand Oaks, CA: Corwin Press.

Bear, D. R., Helman, L., & Woessner, L. (2009). Word study assessment and instruction with English learners in a second grade classroom: Bending with students' growth. In J. Coppola and E. V. Primas (Eds.) *One classroom, many learners: Best literacy practices for today's multilingual classrooms* (pp. 11–40). Newark, DE: International Reading Association.

Bear, D. R., Invernizzi, M., Templeton, S., & Johnston, F. (2012). *Words their way: Word study for phonics, vocabulary, and spelling instruction* (5th ed.). Boston: Pearson/Allyn & Bacon.

Bernhardt, E. (2000). Second-language reading as a case study of reading scholarship in the 20th century. In M. L. Kamil, P. B. Mosenthal,

P. D. Pearson, & R. Barr (Eds.), *Handbook of reading research: Volume III* (pp. 793–811). Mahwah, NJ: Erlbaum.

Berninger, V. W., Cartwright, A. C., Yates, C. M., Swanson, H. L., & Abbott, R. D. (1994). Developmental skills related to writing and reading acquisition in the intermediate grades: Shared and unique functional systems. *Reading and Writing: An Interdisciplinary Journal, 6,* 161–196.

Brock, C., Lapp, D., Salas, R., & Townsend, D. (2009). The case of Ying: The members of a teacher study group learn about fostering the reading comprehension of English learners. In L. Helman (Ed.) *Literacy Development with English Learners: Research-Based Instruction in Grades K-6* (pp. 178–195). New York: The Guilford Press.

California Department of Education. (1997). *California standards for the teaching profession.* Sacramento, CA: CDE Publications.

Calkins, L. (2005). *The nuts and bolts of teaching writing.* Portsmouth, NH: Heinemann.

Calkins, L. (2011). *A curricular plan for the writing workshop.* Portsmouth, NH: Heinemann.

Cantwell, M. (1993, November 2). Editorial notebook: "I am a storyteller": An afternoon with Federico Fellini. *New York Times*

Capps, R., Fix, M., Murray, J., Ost, J., Passel, J. S., & Herwantoro, S. (2005). *The new demography of America's schools: Immigration and the NCLB act.* Washington, DC: Urban Institute. Retrieved from http://www.urban.org/template.cfm?Template=/TaggedContent/ViewPublication.cfm&PublicationID=9452&NavMenuID=95/

Chavis, D. M., Hogge, J. H., McMillan, D. W., & Wandersman, A. (1986). Sense of community through Brunswick's lens: A first look. *Journal of Community Psychology, 14*(1), 24–40.

Clay, M. (2006). *An observation survey of early literacy achievement* (2nd ed.). Portsmouth, NH: Heinemann.

Clay, M. (2010). *Running records for classroom teachers.* Portsmouth, NH: Heinemann.

Council of Chief State School Officers. (2010). *Common core state standards.* Retrieved from http://www.corestandards.org/the-standards/

Cummins, J. (1979). Cognitive/academic language proficiency, linguistic interdependence, the optimum age question, and some other matters. *Working Papers on Bilingualism, 19,* 121–129.

Cummins, J. (1981). The role of primary language development in promoting educational success for language minority students. In California State Department of Education (Ed.), *Schooling and language minority students: A theoretical framework.* Los Angeles: Evaluation, Dissemination and Assessment Center, California State University.

DeNicolo, C. P., & Franquiz, M. E. (2006). "Do I have to say it?" Critical encounters with multicultural children's literature. *Language Arts, 84*(2), 157–170.

Dutro, S., & Helman, L. (2009). Explicit language instruction: A key to constructing meaning. In L. Helman (Ed.), *Literacy development with English learners: Research-based instruction in grades K–6* (pp. 40–63). New York: Guilford Press.

Ehri, L. C. (1997). Learning to read and learning to spell are one and the same, almost. In C. A. Perfetti, L. Rieben, & M. Fayol (Eds.), *Learning to spell: Research, theory, and practice across languages* (pp. 237–269). Mahwah, NJ: Erlbaum.

Fillmore, L. W., & Snow, C. E. (2002). What teachers need to know about language. In C. T. Adger, C. E. Snow, & D. Christian (Eds.), *What teachers need to know about language* (pp. 7–54). Washington, DC, and McHenry, IL: Center for Applied Linguistics and Delta Systems Co., Inc.

Foorman, B. R., & Connor, C. M. (2011). Primary grade reading. In M. L. Kamil, P. D. Pearson, E. B. Moje, & P. P. Afflerbach (Eds.), *Handbook of reading research* (Vol. IV, pp. 136–156). New York: Routledge.

Genesee, F., Lindholm-Leary, K., Saunders, W., & Christian, D. (2005). English language learners in U.S. schools: An overview of research findings. *Journal of Education for Students Placed at Risk, 10*(4), 363–385.

Goldenberg, C. (in press). Research on English learner instruction. In M.Calderón (Ed.), *Evidence-based instruction for English learners.* Bloomington, IN: Solution Tree Press.

Gonzáles, N., Moll, L., & Amanti, C. (2005). *Funds of knowledge: Theorizing practices in households, communities, and classrooms.* Mahwah, NJ: Erlbaum.

Goodman, S. E. (2001). *Ultimate field trip 5: Blasting off to space academy.* New York: Atheneum Books for Young Readers.

Graves, M. (2006). *The vocabulary book: Learning and instruction.* New York: Teachers College Press.

Harvey, S., & Daniels, H. (2009). *Comprehension and collaboration.* Portsmouth, NH: Heinemann.

Helman, L. A. (2005). Spanish speakers learning to read in English: What a large-scale assessment suggests about their progress. In B. Maloch, J. Hoffman, D. Schallert, C. Fairbanks, & J. Worthy (Eds.), *54th yearbook of the National Reading Conference* (pp. 211–226). Oak Creek, WI: National Reading Conference.

Helman, L. (2008). English words needed: Creating research-based vocabulary instruction for English learners. In A. E. Farstrup & S. J. Samuels (Eds.), *What research has to say about vocabulary instruction* (pp. 211–237). Newark, DE: International Reading Association.

Helman, L. (2009). *Literacy development with English learners: Research-based instruction in grades K–6.* New York: Guilford Press.

Helman, L. A., & Bear, D. R. (2007). Does an established model of orthographic development hold true for English learners? In D. W. Rowe,

R. Jimenez, D. L. Compton, D. K. Dickinson, Y. Kim, K. M. Leander, & V. J. Risko (Eds.), *56th yearbook of the National Reading Conference* (pp. 266–280). Oak Creek, WI: National Reading Conference.

Helman, L., Bear, D. R., Invernizzi, M., Templeton, S., & Johnston, F. (2009a). *Emergent sorts for Spanish-speaking English learners.* Boston: Pearson/Allyn & Bacon.

Helman, L., Bear, D. R., Invernizzi, M., Templeton, S., & Johnston, F. (2009b). *Letter name-alphabetic sorts for Spanish-speaking English learners.* Boston: Pearson/Allyn & Bacon.

Helman, L., Bear, D. R., Templeton, S., Invernizzi, M., & Johnston, F. (2012). *Words their way with English learners: Word study for phonics, vocabulary, and spelling* (2nd ed.). Boston: Allyn & Bacon.

Helman, L., & Coffino, K. (2010, April). *Differentiating literacy and content instruction for diverse learners in a rural midwestern school district.* Paper presented at the annual conference of the American Educational Research Association, Denver, CO.

Helman, L., Magnuson, P., & Marx, M. (2008, March). *What are the instructional practices of accomplished reading teachers of English learners?* Paper presented at the annual conference of the American Educational Research Association, Atlanta, GA.

Henderson, E. H. (1990). *Teaching spelling* (2nd ed.). Boston: Houghton Mifflin.

Henderson, A. T., Mapp, K. L., Johnson, V. R., & Davies, D. (2007). *Beyond the bake sale: The essential guide to family–school partnerships.* New York: New Press.

Herrera, S. (2010). *Biography-driven culturally responsive teaching.* New York: Teachers College Press.

Honigsfeld, A., & Dove, M. G. (2010). *Collaboration and co-teaching: Strategies for English learners.* Thousand Oaks, CA: Corwin Press.

Kugler, E. G. (2011). Is anyone listening to families' dreams? *Educational Leadership, 68*(8), 32–36.

Landry, S. H., & Smith, K. E. (2006). The influence of parenting on emerging literacy skills. In D. K. Dickinson & S. B. Neuman (Eds.), *Handbook of early literacy research* (Vol. II, pp. 135–148). New York: Guilford Press.

Lesaux, N., & Geva, E. (2006). Synthesis: Development of literacy in language-minority students. In D. August & T. Shanahan (Eds.), *Developing literacy in second-language learners* (pp. 53–74). Mahwah, NJ: Lawrence Erlbaum.

Lipson, M., & Wixson, K. (2009). *Assessment & instruction of reading and writing difficulties: An interactive approach* (4th ed.). Boston: Allyn & Bacon.

Mapp, K. L. (2003). Having their say: Parents describe why and how they are engaged in their children's learning. *The School Community Journal, 13*(1), 35–64.

Marzano, R., Marzano, J., & Pickering, D. (2003). *Classroom management that works: Research-based strategies for every teacher*. Alexandria, VA: Association for Supervision and Curriculum Development.

McCabe, A. (1997). Cultural background and storytelling: A review and implications for schooling. *The Elementary School Journal, 97*, 453–473.

McCabe, A., & Bliss, L. S. (2003). *Patterns of narrative discourse: A multicultural, life span approach*. Boston: Allyn & Bacon.

Miller, E. T. (2010). An interrogation of the "if only" mentality: One teacher's deficit perspective put on trial. *Early Childhood Education*. doi: 10.1007/s10643-010-0423-z

Minnesota Board of Teaching. (2009). *8710.2000 Standards Of Effective Practice For Teachers*. State of Minnesota: Revisor of Statutes. Available at https://www.revisor.mn.gov/rules/?id=8710.2000

Minnesota Department of Education. (2011). *2011 Minnesota math and reading assessment scores released*. Available at http://education.state.mn.us/mde/index.html

Morris, D., Bloodgood, J. W., Lomax, R. G., & Perney, J. (2003). Developmental steps in learning to read: A longitudinal study in kindergarten and first grade. *Reading Research Quarterly, 38*(3), 302–328.

National Reading Panel. (2000). *Report of the National Reading Panel—Teaching children to read: An evidence-based assessment of the scientific research literature on reading and its implications for reading instruction* (Report of the subgroups). Washington, DC: National Institute of Child Health and Human Development.

New York State Education Department. (2011, September). New York State Teaching Standards. Retrieved from www.highered.nysed.gov/tcert/resteachers/teachingstandards.html

Northeast Foundation for Children. (2011). *Responsive classroom*. Turner Falls, MA: Author. Retrieved from http://www.responsiveclassroom.org/about-responsive-classroom

Ogle, D. M. (1986). K-W-L: A teaching model that develops active reading of expository text. *Reading Teacher, 39*, 564–570.

PeacePartners. (2011). *PeaceBuilders*. Long Beach, CA: Author. Retrieved from http://www.peacebuilders.com/whatWeDo/peaceBuildersProgram.php

Performance Assessment for California Teachers. (2010). *Academic language for elementary literacy*. Retrieved from http://www.pacttpa.org/_main/hub.php?pageName=Teaching_Event_Handbooks#Handbooks

Pinnell, G. S., & Fountas, I. C. (2007). *The continuum of literacy learning: Grades K–8*. Portsmouth, NH: Heinemann.

Pressley, M. (2006). *Reading instruction that works: The case for balanced teaching* (3rd ed.). New York: Guilford Press.

Read, C. (1971). Preschool children's knowledge of English phonology. *Harvard Educational Review, 41*, 1–34.

Saint Paul Public Schools. (2010). *Collaboration: Information and resources about ELL collaboration in SPPS.* Retrieved from http://ell.spps.org/Collaboration.html

Saunders, W. M., Foorman, B. R., & Carlson, C. D. (2006). Is a separate block of time for oral English language development in programs for English learners needed? *The Elementary School Journal, 107*(2), 181–198.

Saunders, W. M., & Goldenberg, C. (2010). Research to guide English Language Development instruction. In D. Dolson & L. Burnham-Massey (Eds.) *Improving education for English learners: Research-based approaches* (pp. 21–81). Sacramento, CA: CDE Press.

Schleppegrell, M. J. (2004). *The language of schooling: A functional linguistics perspective.* Mahwah, NJ: Erlbaum.

Scarcella, R. (2003). *Accelerating academic English: A focus on the English learner.* Oakland, CA: Regents of the University of California.

Snow, C. E., Burns, M. S., & Griffin, P. (1998). *Preventing reading difficulties in young children.* Washington, D. C: National Academy Press.

Snow, M. A. & Katz, A. M. (2010). English language development: Foundations and implementation in kindergarten through grade five. In California Department of Education. *Improving education for English learners: Research-based approaches.* (pp. 83-148). Sacramento, CA: California Department of Education.

Stauffer, R. (1980). *The language-experience approach to the teaching of reading* (2nd ed.). New York: Harper & Row.

Thomas, W. P., & Collier, V. P. (2002). *A national study of school effectiveness for language minority students' long-term academic achievement.* Santa Cruz, CA: Center for Research on Education, Diversity and Excellence. Retrieved from http://crede.berkeley.edu/research/crede/research/llaa/1.1_final.html

Trumbull, E. & Farr, B. (2005). *Language and learning: What teachers need to know.* Norwood, MA: Christopher-Gordon Publishers.

Uribe, M., & Nathenson-Mejía, S. (2008). *Literacy essentials for English language learners: Successful transitions.* New York: Teachers College Press.

U.S. Department of Education. (2004). National Center for Education Statistics, schools and staffing survey, 2003–04, public school, BIA school, and private school data files. Retrieved from http://nces.ed.gov/surveys/sass/tables/sass_2004_06.asp

U.S. Department of Education. (2010). Institute of Education Sciences, National Center for Education Statistics, National Assessment of Educational Progress, 1998, 2000, 2002, 2003, 2005, 2007, and 2009 reading assessments. Retrieved from http://nationsreportcard.gov/reading_2009/nat_g4.asp?subtab_id=Tab_7&tab_id=tab1#tabsContainer

Valencia, S. & Buly, M. R. (2004). Behind test scores: What struggling readers really need. *The Reading Teacher, 57*(6), 520–531.

Weinstein, C., Curran, M., & Tomlinson-Clarke, S. (2003). Culturally responsive classroom management: Awareness into action. *Theory into Practice, 42*(4), 269–276.

White, E. B. (1945). *Stuart Little* (G. Williams, Illus.). New York: Harper & Row.

Wolfersberger, M. E., Reutzel, D. R., Sudweeks, R., & Fawson, P. C. (2004). Developing and validating the Classroom Literacy Environmental Profile (CLEP): A tool for examining the "print richness" of early childhood and elementary classrooms. *Journal of Literacy Research 36*(2), 83–144.

World-Class Instructional Design and Assessment [WIDA] Consortium. (2011, September). Defining features of academic language. Retrieved from http://www.wida.us/standards/elp.aspx

Zwiers, J. (2008). *Building academic language: Essential practices for content classrooms*. San Francisco: Jossey-Bass.

Index

About the Author

Lori Helman, Ph.D., is Associate Professor at the University of Minnesota in the Department of Curriculum and Instruction and Co-Director of the Minnesota Center for Reading Research. She specializes in literacy education and teacher leadership. Formerly an elementary bilingual classroom teacher, she was also a coordinator of beginning teacher development and literacy coordinator of her school district. She has expertise in working with students from culturally and linguistically diverse backgrounds, and her research focuses on the instructional practices that best serve diverse elementary students. She is lead author of *Words Their Way with English Learners: Word Study for Phonics, Vocabulary, and Spelling* and companion sorting texts that differentiate word study for English learners. She teaches courses in the assessment of reading difficulties, instruction for struggling readers, and the literacy development of English learners. She currently is co-directing a school reform project being implemented in a large urban city.